4 ★ All-Star

Post-Testing Study Guide

Linda Lee ★ Kristin Sherman ★ Stephen Sloan ★
Grace Tanaka ★ Shirley Velasco

McGraw-Hill

All-Star 4 Post-Testing Study Guide

ISBN 13: 978-0-07-313812-1
ISBN 10: 0-07-313812-6
1 2 3 4 5 6 7 8 9   QPD/QPD   11 10 09 08 07 06

Editorial director: Erik Gundersen
Developmental editor: Karen P. Hazar
Production manager: Juanita Thompson
Interior designer: Wee Design Group
Cover designer: Wee Design Group
Illustrators: Burgundy Beam, Andrew Lange, Rich Stergulz, Carlotta Tormey
Photo Credits: All photos are courtesy of Getty Images Royalty Free Collection and the CORBIS Royalty-Free Collection with the exception of the following: page 9 © David MacDonald/PhotoEdit; page 10 © Camille Tokerud/Getty Images; page 29 © David N. Averbach; page 31 © Jim Naughten/Getty Images; page 32 © ImageState/PictureQuest; page 40 © McGraw-Hill Companies, Inc./Gary He, photographer; page 57 © Brand X Pictures/PictureQuest; page 58 © Rob Melnychuk/Getty Images; page 68 © Brand X Pictures/Getty Images; page 80 top: © Tony Freeman/PhotoEdit, Inc.; page 80 bottom: © Chabruken/Getty Images; page 95, milk: © Ryan McVay/Getty Images; page 95, parking meter: © Brand X Pictures/PunchStock.

McGraw-Hill

The *McGraw-Hill* Companies

Contents

About This Book iv

About the Correlation Chart v

Correlation Chart vi

Unit 1   Skills and Abilities 1

Unit 2   Getting Around 12

Unit 3   Your Health 23

Unit 4   Rights and Responsibilities 38

Unit 5   Consumer News and Views 51

Unit 6   Rules and Laws 65

Unit 7   Career Paths 78

Unit 8   Money Matters 91

BEST *Plus* Descriptors and Practice Questions 104

About This Book

Welcome to the All-Star 4 Post-Testing Study Guide. This book provides instructors and administrators with reproducible sample work and information that can be used to help document student readiness for post-testing.

The book has four features:

- All-Star correlation spreadsheet for LCP Level E, BEST *Plus,* and CASAS
- Sample competency documents for portfolio use
- Additional documents to correspond to assessment needs
- BEST *Plus* chart with descriptors and practice questions

The activities from All-Star 4 and the additional documents address the competencies as indicated on the vertical description line of each page. These activities can be used as sample work for student portfolios, and as readiness indicators for post-testing.

About the Correlation Chart

On the following pages, you will find the Correlation Chart for the All-Star 4 Post-Testing Study Guide. This chart will guide you not only in using the reproducible pages in this book, but also in using the components in the All-Star series to prepare your students for post-testing, and to compile a portfolio to be used for fulfilling competency requirements.

This short but comprehensive guide to using the Correlation Chart will lead you through the chart column by column, allowing you to use this material to best prepare your students for competency and standards testing.

Descriptors

Beginning with the left hand column, you will see a column titled *Descriptor.* This *Descriptor* column contains the competency or standard for which each particular row will provide detailed information. If you are using BEST *Plus*, you will note the descriptor language in italics with a BEST *Plus* indication.

Standards

The next three columns are particular to standards and competencies used across the United States. The second column in the Correlation Chart covers LCP (Literacy Completion Points). Reading down this column, you will see a numbered code indicating which LCP standard a particular *Descriptor* applies to. Continuing to travel to the right, you'll see the following column is titled CASAS (Comprehensive Adult Student Assessment System). Again, reading down this column, you will see a numbered code indicating which CASAS standard a particular *Descriptor* fits. The third column covers BEST *Plus* testing. Reading down this column, you will see a check mark to indicate that the *Descriptor* matches BEST *Plus* language testing.

Correlations and Study Guide Pages

The next three columns are titled SB (Student Book), WB (Workbook), and TE (Teacher's Edition). Under each of these columns, you will find page numbers. These page numbers indicate the pages in each component that fulfill a particular competency or standard. The final column on the right points you to the page in this All-Star 4 Post-Testing Study Guide that covers the *Descriptor* listed in that row.

To the BEST *Plus* Instructor

The All-Star 4 Post-Testing Study Guide correlation chart will point you to pages in the All-Star 4 Student Book, Workbook, and Teacher's Edition that offer exercises and activities covering a wide range of topics and skills to help students prepare for the BEST *Plus*.

On many All-Star 4 Study Guide pages, you will find BEST *Plus* practice questions to use in helping students prepare for the test. In addition, at the back of this Study Guide, you will find a separate list of practice questions similar to those that may appear on the BEST *Plus* test.

Correlation Chart

Pre-Unit: Getting Started

DESCRIPTOR	LCP	CASAS	BEST+	SB	WB	TE	SG
Paraphrase passages, words, or ideas in conversations. *BEST Plus: Identify self and share personal information. State information about country of origin and current residence.*	83.02		✓	Pg. 3		Pg. 3	
Apply oral communication skills to simple interviews and presentations.	83.04	4.1.5 4.1.7		Pg. 3		Pg. 3	
Understand use of formal versus informal vocabulary, reductions, and basic idiomatic expressions.	83.03		✓	Pg. 2		Pg. 2	
Demonstrate ability to use textbooks effectively (headings, table of contents, index).	83.11			Pg. 3		Pg. 3	

Unit 1: Skills and Abilities

DESCRIPTOR	LCP	CASAS	BEST+	SB	WB	TE	SG
Describe personal career goals, interests, and review jobs including LPN, typist. *BEST Plus: Discuss learning new skills and interests. Describe learning goals and best ways to learn new things. Identify self and share personal information about country of origin and current residence.*	69.01	4.1.4 4.1.8 4.4.5 7.1.1	✓	Pgs. 4, 5, **19**	Pgs. 2, 3	Pgs. 5, 6, 16, 18, 23, 183, 184	1
Demonstrate standards of behavior for job interview; ask and answer questions during a job interview; write a thank you note; conduct a follow-up call after a simulated job interview. *BEST Plus: Discuss emotional state of being about job interviews.*	69.04	4.1.5 4.4.1 4.4.3 4.6.2	✓	Pgs. 14, 15, **21**	Pg. 17	Pgs. 18, 24	2
Demonstrate understanding of U.S. work ethic (appropriate behavior, attire, attitudes, and social interactions that affect job performance).	70.01	4.2.4 4.4.1 4.4.6		Pgs. 6, 14, 16	Pg. 5	Pgs. 7, 8, 17, 18, 20	
Demonstrate basic problem–solving skills in the workplace.	70.02	7.3.4		Pgs. 6, 7	Pg. 5	Pgs. 7, 8	
Explore options regarding on-the-job opportunities and continuing education to acquire higher-level skills and promotions.	71.01	4.4.2 4.4.4		Pgs. 4, 5	Pgs. 2, 3, 19	Pgs. 5, 6, 16, 18, 183, 184	
Demonstrate knowledge of operating equipment necessary for home and work.	72.01			Pgs. 8, 9	Pgs. 13, 15	Pgs. 14, 19, 24, 25, 27	
Identify and explain common problems and solutions.	73.02	7.3.1 7.3.2 7.3.3		Pg. 6	Pgs. 12, 13	Pgs. 8, 25	
Demonstrate ability to take and report accurate messages.	74.01	2.1.7		Pg. **8**	Pgs. 6, 7	Pgs. 9, 11, 12	3

Legend:
SB = Student Book   **WB** = Workbook   **TE** = Teacher's Edition   **SG** = Study Guide   **LCP** = Literacy Completion Point
CASAS = Comprehensive Adult Student Assessment System   **BEST+** = Basic English Skills Test, Updated

Unit 1 (continued)

DESCRIPTOR	LCP	CASAS	BEST+	SB	WB	TE	SG
Demonstrate ability to give and request information clearly by telephone.	74.02	2.1.8		Pgs. 8, 9	Pgs. 6, 7	Pgs. 9, 11, 12	
Demonstrate knowledge of U.S. educational system (compulsory schooling, child care, PTA).	82.01	2.5.5 2.5.9			Pgs. **12**, 13	Pg. 25	4
Develop awareness of acceptable/unacceptable parenting and disciplinary practices.	82.03	3.5.7			Pgs. 12, 13	Pg. 25	
Paraphrase passages, words, or ideas in conversations. *BEST Plus: State the date of your birthday.*	83.02		✓	Pg. 12	Pgs. 7, 10	Pgs. 15, 16, 183	
Apply oral communication skills to simple interviews and presentations.	83.04	4.1.5 4.1.7		Pgs. 6, 7, **14**		Pgs. 7, 8, 9, 17, 18, 19	5
Utilize new vocabulary by context.	83.06			Pgs. 6, 7, 17	Pgs. 3, 4, 5, 8, 13	Pgs. 7, 13, 21, 25	
Recognize sequence of events in a reading passage.	83.07			Pg. 8	Pg. 6	Pg. 9	
Recognize style and tone in a reading passage.	83.08			Pg. 20	Pgs. 20, 21	Pg. 24	
Distinguish fact from opinion (inference). *BEST Plus: State reasons for immigrating to the U.S. and why someone would want to become a citizen of the U.S.*	83.12	7.2.4	✓	Pgs. **18**, 19	Pg. 18	Pg. 23	6
Interpret statistical information from diagrams, tables, graphs, charts, and schedules.	83.13	6.6.5		Pgs. 4, 14			
Skim and scan to locate information.	83.14			Pgs. **10**, 11, 14, 19	Pgs. 15, 19	Pgs. 13, 23, 27	7
Write a paragraph focusing on one topic (narration, definition, description, cause and effect).	83.15			Pgs. 20, 21	Pgs. 20, 21	Pgs. 13, 22, 24, 26	
Write complex and compound sentences with correct terminology and punctuation.	83.16			Pgs. 10, 12, 13	Pgs. 2, 8, 11	Pgs. 14, 15	
Demonstrate ability to apply a variety of test–taking strategies (multiple choice, true/false, cloze, short essays).	83.18	7.4.7		Pgs. 16, 17	Pgs. **16**, **17**	Pgs. 20, 21	8, 9
Use verbs: past continuous, past perfect, modals.	84.01		✓		Pg. 7		
Identify parts of speech and use in sentences.	84.02				Pg. **4**		10
Use consonant blends, diphthongs, and digraphs.	85.02		✓	Pg. **15**		Pg. 18	11

Legend:
SB = Student Book   WB = Workbook   TE = Teacher's Edition   SG = Study Guide   LCP = Literacy Completion Point
CASAS = Comprehensive Adult Student Assessment System   BEST+ = Basic English Skills Test, Updated

Correlation Chart

Unit 2: Getting Around

DESCRIPTOR	LCP	CASAS	BEST+	SB	WB	TE	SG
Demonstrate knowledge of operating equipment necessary for home and work. *BEST Plus: Describe reasons for choosing particular transportation methods.*	72.01		✓	Pg. 22	Pgs. 25, 33, 35	Pgs. 33, 39, 49, 51	
Ask for and provide directions and instructions.	73.01	4.6.1			Pgs. **29**, 34, 35	Pgs. 51, 52	12
Identify and explain common problems and solutions.	73.02	7.3.1 7.3.2 7.3.3		Pgs. 22, 24, 32, 33	Pgs. **30**, **31**	Pgs. 31, 32, 33, 42, 43, 46	13, 14
Demonstrate ability to take and report accurate messages.	74.01	2.1.7		Pg. 26		Pg. 36	
Follow emergency procedures and complete medical forms and accident reports.	75.02	3.2.1		Pgs. **32**, **33**	Pgs. 22, 23	Pg. 42	15
Demonstrate understanding of time zones.	76.03	2.1.3			Pg. 28		
Compare/contrast basic factors when planning a trip (distance, cost, tips, comfort and convenience). *BEST Plus: Describe how you choose a method of transportation.*	77.01	1.1.3 1.2.2 1.9.3 1.9.4 2.2.4 2.2.5 2.6.3	✓	Pgs. 26, **28**, 29, 34	Pgs. 26, 27, 28	Pgs. 34, 38, 44	16
Discuss U.S. driving responsibilities and driver's license exam with emphasis on auto insurance (driver's license, traffic regulations, insurance, seat belts, child safety restraints). *BEST Plus: Describe driving/seatbelt safety and safety of children.*	77.02	1.9.1 1.9.2 1.9.8 2.2.1 2.2.2	✓	Pgs. 22, 23, 24, 25, 26, 34, **188**	Pgs. 22, 23, 24, 25, 30, 36, 37, 40, 41	Pgs. 30, 31, 32, 33, 36, 37, 44, 45, 185	17
Demonstrate appropriate response when stopped by law enforcement officers.	77.03	1.9.7 5.3.5		Pgs. 22, 23, 26, 27		Pgs. 30, 31, 36, 37, 45, 186	
Describe a problem/request service (emergency road assistance, car accident, auto maintenance, and vehicle theft). *BEST Plus: State opinion about drivers in the U.S. and how they compare to drivers in country of origin.*	77.04	1.9.6 1.9.7	✓	Pgs. 22, 23, 32, 33	Pgs. 22, 23, 24, 37	Pgs. 30, 31, 32, 36, 37, 40, 42, 45, 46	
Compare/contrast various types of insurance policies (life, health, homeowner's, renter's, vehicle).	79.04	1.4.6 1.9.8 3.2.3		Pgs. **24**, 25	Pgs. 24, 25	Pgs. 32, 33	18
Interpret street maps; local, state, and national maps; and map keys for evacuation procedures.	81.02	1.1.3 1.9.4 2.2.5 4.3.1 6.6.5		Pgs. 28, 29	Pgs. 29, 34, 35	Pgs. 38, 51	

Legend:
SB = Student Book   WB = Workbook   TE = Teacher's Edition   SG = Study Guide   LCP = Literacy Completion Point
CASAS = Comprehensive Adult Student Assessment System   BEST+ = Basic English Skills Test, Updated

Unit 2 (continued)

DESCRIPTOR	LCP	CASAS	BEST+	SB	WB	TE	SG
Listen and follow directions.	83.01	2.5.4			Pgs. 29, 34, 35	Pg. 51	
Apply oral communication skills to simple interviews and presentations.	83.04	4.1.5 4.1.7		Pgs. 24, 26, 28	Pgs. 23, 33, 35	Pgs. 31, 32, 33, 37, 38, 39, 42, 49, 51	
Comprehend selected reading passages recognizing the main idea.	83.05			Pgs. 36, 37	Pgs. **38**, 39	Pg. 47	19
Utilize new vocabulary by context.	83.06		✓	Pgs. 24, 35	Pgs. 24, 25, 40	Pgs. 32, 45	
Recognize sequence of events in a reading passage.	83.07				Pg. 26	Pg. 34	
Demonstrate the ability to use the dictionary.	83.09	7.4.5		Pg. 24		Pg. 32	
Distinguish fact from opinion (inference).	83.12	7.2.4		Pgs. 22, 23		Pg. 30	
Interpret statistical information from diagrams, tables, graphs, charts, and schedules.	83.13	6.6.5		Pgs. 26, 27, 28, 29, 32	Pgs. 26, 27, 32, 33	Pgs. 37, 38, 42, 49, 50	
Write a paragraph focusing on one topic (narration, definition, description, cause and effect).	83.15			Pg. 39	Pg. 41	Pg. 48	
Write complex and compound sentences with correct terminology and punctuation.	83.16			Pgs. 30, 31, 38, **39**	Pgs. 30, 41, 42	Pgs. 40, 41, 48, 186	20
Demonstrate ability to apply a variety of test–taking strategies (multiple choice, true/false, cloze, short essays).	83.18	7.4.7		Pgs. 24, 34	Pgs. 36, 37	Pgs. 32, 44, 45	
Use verbs: past continuous, past perfect, modals, conditionals, gerunds, participles, infinitives.	84.01		✓	Pgs. 30,	Pgs. 30, **31**	Pgs. 39, 31, 42, 186	21 40, 41,
Use consonant blends, diphthongs, and digraphs.	85.02		✓	Pg. **33**		Pg. 43	22

Correlation Chart

Unit 3: Your Health

DESCRIPTOR	LCP	CASAS	BEST+	SB	WB	TE	SG
Use a variety of resources to search for job opportunities and discuss required training.	69.02	4.1.3 4.1.4 4.4.5			Pgs. 52, 53	Pg. 73	
Identify OSHA safety procedures at work.	70.05				Pgs. **52, 53**	Pg. 73	23, 24
Demonstrate knowledge of operating equipment necessary for home and work.	72.01				Pgs. 45, 53, 55	Pgs. 73, 74	
Demonstrate ability to take and report accurate messages.	74.01	2.1.7		Pgs. 44, 52		Pgs. 59, 68, 69	
Demonstrate ability to give and request information clearly by telephone.	74.02	2.1.8		Pg. 44	Pgs. **46,** 47	Pg. 61	25
Communicate effectively using vocabulary related to doctors, dentists, body parts, illnesses, and medications. *BEST Plus: Describe similarities and differences between going to the doctor in the U.S. versus country of origin.*	75.01	3.1.1 3.1.2 3.1.3	✓	Pgs. 40, 41, **42,** 43, 44, 52	Pgs. 44, 45, 50, 51, 57	Pgs. 54, 56, 57, 58, 59, 67, 68, 70, **188**	26, 27
Follow emergency procedures and complete medical forms and accident reports.	75.02	3.2.1		Pgs. 40, 41, 56	Pgs. 42, **43,** 47	Pgs. 54, 62, 65, 67, 70, 72, 187,188	28
Read and interpret nutritional information listed on food labels and plan balanced diets. *BEST Plus: State opinion about what people can do to stay healthy. State opinion about exercise.*	75.03	3.3.1 3.3.2	✓	Pgs. **46,** 47, 51, 52	Pgs. 48, **49,** 56, 59	Pgs. 63, 67, 68	29, 30
Recognize problems related to substance/drug abuse, and identify where treatment may be obtained. *BEST Plus: State opinion about illicit drug use among American teens and how to educate people about drugs.*	75.04	2.5.3 3.3.1 3.3.3 3.4.5	✓		Pgs. **54,** 55	Pgs. 74, 75	31
Recognize requirements for immunizations.	75.05	3.2.2		Pgs. **50, 51**		Pgs. 66, 67	32
Report detrimental health and safety conditions in private and public places.	78.01	1.4.7 1.4.8 4.3.4			Pgs. 52, 53	Pg. 73	
Compare/contrast various types of insurance policies (life, health, homeowner's, renter's, vehicle).	79.04	1.4.6 1.9.8 3.2.3			Pgs. 47, **60**		33
Read and discuss information related to current events.	80.05	2.6.2 2.7.6 6.8.1			Pgs. 48, 55	Pg. 74	
Paraphrase passages, words, or ideas in conversations.	83.02			Pg. 44	Pg. 50	Pgs. 55, 61, 63	
Apply oral communication skills to simple interviews and presentations.	83.04	4.1.5 4.1.7		Pgs. 44, 46	Pg. 53	Pgs. 61, 63, 73	

Legend:
SB = Student Book   WB = Workbook   TE = Teacher's Edition   SG = Study Guide   LCP = Literacy Completion Point
CASAS = Comprehensive Adult Student Assessment System   BEST+ = Basic English Skills Test, Updated

Unit 3 (continued)

DESCRIPTOR	LCP	CASAS	BEST+	SB	WB	TE	SG
Utilize new vocabulary by context.	83.06			Pgs. 53, 54, **55**	Pgs. 58, 59	Pgs. 66, 69, 71	34
Recognize sequence of events in a reading passage.	83.07			Pg. 40	Pg. 46	Pg. 54	
Demonstrate the ability to use the dictionary.	83.09	7.4.5		Pg. 50	Pg. 58		
Preview and make predictions prior to reading.	83.10				Pg. 59		
Interpret statistical information from diagrams, tables, graphs, charts, and schedules.	83.13	6.6.5		Pgs. 45, 51	Pgs. 46, **55**	Pgs. 59, 66, 74	35
Skim and scan to locate information.	83.14			Pgs. 42, 46, 50, 51	Pgs. 43, 49, 54	Pgs. 56, 63, 66, 74	
Write a paragraph focusing on one topic (narration, definition, description, cause and effect).	83.15				Pg. **61**	Pg. 70	36
Write complex and compound sentences with correct terminology and punctuation.	83.16			Pgs. 48, 49, **56**, 57	Pgs. 42, 50, 60, 61	Pgs. 64, 65, 72, 73, 187	37
Demonstrate ability to apply a variety of test–taking strategies (multiple choice, true/false, cloze, short essays).	83.18	7.4.7		Pg. 52	Pgs. 56, 57	Pgs. 65, 67, 68, 69, 187, 188	
Use past tense verbs.	84.01		✓		Pg. 42		
Identify parts of speech and use in sentences.	84.02			Pgs. 48, 49		Pg. 64	
Use stress and intonation in phrases and sentences.	85.01		✓			Pg. 57	

Unit 4: Rights and Responsibilities

DESCRIPTOR	LCP	CASAS	BEST+	SB	WB	TE	SG
Demonstrate understanding of job specifications, policies, standards, benefits, and W2 and W4 forms. Complete sample W4 form; wages, deductions, and timekeeping forms.	69.05	4.1.1 4.2.1 4.2.3 4.4.4		Pgs. 73, **189**		Pg. 94	38
Demonstrate understanding of worker's rights (compensation, unionization, right to work).	70.04	4.2.2		Pgs. 58, 59, 60, **68**, **69**, 73	Pg. 76	Pgs. 77, 79, 88, 89, 92, 93, 94, 190	39
Identify OSHA safety procedures at work.	70.05			Pgs. 64, 65	Pg. 69	Pg. 85	
Explore options regarding on-the-job opportunities and continuing education to acquire higher-level skills and promotions.	71.01	4.4.2 4.4.4		Pgs. 63, 69		Pg. 90	
Demonstrate knowledge of operating equipment necessary for home and work.	72.01				Pgs. 73, 75	Pgs. 86, 96, 97	
Identify and explain common problems and solutions.	73.02	7.3.1 7.3.2 7.3.3			Pg. **72**	Pg. 96	40

Legend:
SB = Student Book   WB = Workbook   TE = Teacher's Edition   SG = Study Guide   LCP = Literacy Completion Point
CASAS = Comprehensive Adult Student Assessment System   BEST+ = Basic English Skills Test, Updated

Correlation Chart

Unit 4 (continued)

DESCRIPTOR	LCP	CASAS	BEST+	SB	WB	TE	SG
Demonstrate ability to take and report accurate messages. *BEST Plus: State opinion about how children learn and what is important to learn at school.*	74.01	2.1.7	✓	Pg. 62		Pgs. 81, 82	
Read and discuss rental agreements/contracts and renter/landlord rights and responsibilities.	79.02	1.4.3 1.4.4 1.4.5 1.4.7			Pg. 72	Pg. 96	
Demonstrate understanding of selected U.S. historical traditions and common social customs.	80.01	2.7.1 2.7.2 2.7.3	✓	Pgs. 58, 59, 60, 61, 66, 67, 70	Pgs. 63, 64, **65**, 67, 70, 71, 74, 75, 77, 78, 79	Pgs. 77, 78, 79, 80, 87, 88, 91, 97, 189	41
Interact with community services, organizations, and government agencies.	80.02	2.5.2 2.5.3 2.5.5 2.5.6 2.5.9	✓	Pgs. 64, 65, 70	Pgs. 68, **69**, 78, 79	Pgs. 84, 85, 91	42
Demonstrate ability to interact with local, state, and national officials and their functions.	80.03	5.5.8		Pgs. 74, **75**	Pgs. 78, 79, 81	Pg. 95	43
Read and discuss information related to current events.	80.05	2.6.2 2.7.6 6.8.1			Pg. 77		
Interpret street maps; local, state, and national maps; and map keys for evacuation procedures.	81.02	1.1.3 1.9.4 2.2.5 4.3.1 6.6.5			Pg. 62		
Demonstrate knowledge of U.S. educational system (compulsory schooling, child care, PTA). *BEST Plus: State opinion about how children learn and what is important to learn at school.*	82.01	2.5.5 2.5.9	✓	Pgs. **62**, 63, 70	Pgs. **66**, 67	Pgs. 81, 82, 83, 91	44, 45
Identify means to access educational opportunities for children (special programs, scholarships, extracurricular activities).	82.02	2.5.5		Pgs. 62, 63		Pg. 81	
Develop awareness of acceptable/unacceptable parenting and disciplinary practices.	82.03	3.5.7		Pgs. 62, 63		Pg. 81	
Paraphrase passages, words, or ideas in conversations.	83.02				Pg. 66		
Apply oral communication skills to simple interviews and presentations.	83.04	4.1.5 4.1.7		Pgs. 58, 60, 62, 67	Pg. 78	Pgs. 77, 78, 80, 83, 88, 97	
Utilize new vocabulary by context.	83.06			Pgs. 60, 71	Pgs. 67, **68**	Pgs. 79, 80, 85, 91, 94	46

Legend:
SB = Student Book   WB = Workbook   TE = Teacher's Edition   SG = Study Guide   LCP = Literacy Completion Point
CASAS = Comprehensive Adult Student Assessment System   BEST+ = Basic English Skills Test, Updated

Unit 4 (continued)

DESCRIPTOR	LCP	CASAS	BEST+	SB	WB	TE	SG
Recognize style and tone in a reading passage.	83.08			Pgs. 74, 75	Pgs. 80, 81	Pg. 95	
Preview and make predictions prior to reading.	83.10			Pgs. 64, 68		Pgs. 86, 89	
Distinguish fact from opinion.	83.12	7.2.4				Pg. 78	
Interpret statistical information from diagrams, tables, graphs, charts, and schedules.	83.13	6.6.5		Pgs. 63, 69, 73	Pgs. 63, **77**	Pgs. 79, 81, 90	47
Skim and scan to locate information.	83.14			Pgs. 64, 68, **72**, 73	Pgs. 65, 69, 72, 74, 78	Pgs. 80, 85, 89, 94, 97, 189	48
Write a paragraph focusing on one topic (narration, definition, description, cause and effect).	83.15			Pg. 75		Pgs. 79, 93, 95, 96	
Write complex and compound sentences with correct terminology and punctuation.	83.16				Pg. 63		
Demonstrate ability to apply a variety of test–taking strategies (multiple choice, true/false, cloze, short essays).	83.18	7.4.7		Pgs. 58, 70, 71	Pgs. 76, 77	Pgs. 77, 80, 91, 189	
Identify parts of speech and use in sentences.	84.02				Pg. **64**	Pg. 85	49
Use active and passive voice.	84.03		✓	Pgs. **66**, 67	Pgs. 70, 71	Pgs. 87, 88, 190	50

Unit 5: Consumer News and Views

DESCRIPTOR	LCP	CASAS	BEST+	SB	WB	TE	SG
Demonstrate knowledge of operating equipment necessary for home and work.	72.01				Pg. 95	Pgs. 110, 118	
Ask for and provide directions and instructions.	73.01	4.6.1		Pgs. 80, 81	Pg. 93	Pg. 117	
Identify and explain common problems and solutions.	73.02	7.3.1 7.3.2 7.3.3		Pgs. 80, 81	Pgs. 85, 100, 101		
Demonstrate ability to take and report accurate messages.	74.01	2.1.7		Pgs. 80, 88		Pgs. 103, 105, 113	
Demonstrate ability to give and request information clearly by telephone.	74.02	2.1.8		Pg. 80		Pgs. 103, 105, 111	
Demonstrate understanding of banking system (loans, interest rates, investments, mortgages), terms, foreign currencies, and exchange rates. *BEST Plus: Describe shopping preferences and state opinion about buying clothes. Describe preferences and methods of payment.*	76.01	1.8.1 1.8.2 1.8.4	✓	Pgs. 76, 77	Pgs. **87**, 98, 99	Pg. 100	51
Interpret classified ads and other resources to locate housing (lease or purchase).	79.01	1.4.2 1.4.3		Pgs. **86**, **87**		Pgs. 110, 111	52, 53

Legend:
SB = Student Book   WB = Workbook   TE = Teacher's Edition   SG = Study Guide   LCP = Literacy Completion Point
CASAS = Comprehensive Adult Student Assessment System   BEST+ = Basic English Skills Test, Updated

Correlation Chart

Unit 5 (continued)

DESCRIPTOR	LCP	CASAS	BEST+	SB	WB	TE	SG
Compare/contrast advertisements, labels, and charts to select goods and services. *BEST Plus: Describe shopping preferences, payment, and how TV and newspaper advertisements influence shopping decisions.*	79.03	1.2.1 1.3.1 1.3.5 1.6.1	✓	Pgs. 76, 77, 78, 79, 80, 81, **82**, **83**, 86, 88	Pgs. 82, 83, 84, 86, 87, 88, 89, 96, 97, 98, 99	Pgs. 99, 100, 101, 102, 103, 105, 106, 107, 108, 110, 112, 114, 191, 192	54, 55
Interact with community services, organizations, and government agencies.	80.02	2.5.2 2.5.3 2.5.5 2.5.6 2.5.9			Pgs. **94**, 95	Pg. 118	56
Listen and follow directions.	83.01	2.5.4			Pgs. 92, **93**	Pg. 117	57
Paraphrase passages, words, or ideas in conversations.	83.02			Pgs. 80, 85		Pgs. 105, 109	
Apply oral communication skills to simple interviews and presentations.	83.04	4.1.5 4.1.7		Pgs. 78, 80	Pgs. 93, 95	Pgs. 100, 101, 103, 105, 117, 118	
Utilize new vocabulary by context.	83.06			Pgs. 78, 79, 89		Pgs. 101, 113	
Recognize sequence of events in a reading passage.	83.07				Pg. **86**		58
Demonstrate the ability to use the dictionary.	83.09	7.4.5		Pgs. **90**, **91**		Pg. 115	59, 60
Interpret statistical information from diagrams, tables, graphs, charts, and schedules.	83.13	6.6.5		Pg. 82	Pgs. 92, 93	Pgs. 101, 107, 117	
Skim and scan to locate information.	83.14			Pgs. **92**, 93	Pg. 82	Pgs. 106, 116, 191	61
Write a paragraph focusing on one topic (narration, definition, description, cause and effect).	83.15			Pgs. 87, 92, 93		Pgs. 102, 107, 110, 114, 116	
Write complex and compound sentences with correct terminology and punctuation.	83.16				Pg. **98**	Pgs. 99, 101, 108, 116, 192	62
Demonstrate ability to apply a variety of test–taking strategies (multiple choice, true/false, cloze, short essays).	83.18	7.4.7		Pgs. 88, 89	Pgs. 88, 96, 97	Pgs. 112, 113	
Use verbs: tag questions/answers.	84.01		✓	Pgs. 84, 85	Pgs. **90**, 91		63

Legend:
SB = Student Book   WB = Workbook   TE = Teacher's Edition   SG = Study Guide   LCP = Literacy Completion Point
CASAS = Comprehensive Adult Student Assessment System   BEST+ = Basic English Skills Test, Updated

Unit 5 (continued)

DESCRIPTOR	LCP	CASAS	BEST+	SB	WB	TE	SG
Identify parts of speech and use in sentences.	84.02			Pgs. 84, 85	Pgs. 84, 90, 91, 95	Pgs. 106, 108, 109, 118, 192	
Use stress and intonation in phrases and sentences.	85.01		✓	Pgs. 84, **87**	Pgs. 90, 91	Pgs. 108, 110, 111	64

Unit 6: Rules and Laws

DESCRIPTOR	LCP	CASAS	BEST+	SB	WB	TE	SG
Demonstrate understanding of job specifications, policies, standards, benefits, W2 and W4 forms. Complete sample W4 form; wages, deductions, and timekeeping forms.	69.05	4.1.1 4.2.1 4.2.3 4.4.4			Pgs. 114, 115	Pg. 139	
Demonstrate understanding of worker's rights (compensation, unionization, right to work).	70.04	4.2.2			Pgs. **114,** 115	Pg. 139	65
Demonstrate knowledge of operating equipment necessary for home and work.	72.01				Pgs. 113, 115	Pgs. 120, 131, 138, 139	
Demonstrate ability to take and report accurate messages.	74.01	2.1.7		Pgs. 98, 99		Pgs. 120, 125	
Demonstrate ability to give and request information clearly by telephone.	74.02	2.1.8			Pg. **106**	Pg. 126	66
Discuss U.S. driving responsibilities and driver's license exam with emphasis on auto insurance (driver's license, traffic regulations, insurance, seat belts, child safety restraints).	77.02	1.9.1 1.9.2 1.9.8 2.2.1 2.2.2		Pgs. 98, 100, 101, 106	Pg. **116**	Pgs. 122, 124, 127, 133	67
Demonstrate appropriate response when stopped by law enforcement officers.	77.03	1.9.7 5.3.5		Pgs. 96, 97, 100, 101	Pgs. **108, 109**	Pgs. 122, 127	68, 69
Identify ways of preventing common crimes (i.e. rape, burglary, domestic assault, car theft, etc.). *BEST Plus: State opinion about the degree to which violence on television may promote violent behavior.*	78.02	1.6.2 3.4.2 3.5.9 5.3.7 5.3.8	✓	Pgs. **104, 105,** 190	Pgs. 105, 110	Pg. 131	70
Interact with community services, organizations, and government agencies.	80.02	2.5.2 2.5.3 2.5.5 2.5.6 2.5.9		Pg. 104	Pg. 117	Pg. 131	

Legend:
SB = Student Book   **WB** = Workbook   **TE** = Teacher's Edition   **SG** = Study Guide   **LCP** = Literacy Completion Point
CASAS = Comprehensive Adult Student Assessment System   **BEST+** = Basic English Skills Test, Updated

Correlation Chart

Unit 6 (continued)

DESCRIPTOR	LCP	CASAS	BEST+	SB	WB	TE	SG
Demonstrate understanding of trial by jury and other elements in a U.S. court of law (judge, jury, lawyers, and legal assistance).	80.04	5.1.4 5.3.3 5.5.3 5.5.6 5.6.3		Pgs. **94**, 95, 96, 97, 106	Pgs. 102, 103, 104	Pgs. 120, 121, 122, 123, 126, 128, 130, 133, 134, 135, 193, 194	71
Read and discuss information related to current events.	80.05	2.6.2 2.7.6 6.8.1		Pgs. 96, 97		Pg. 122	
Describe recycling regulations and illegal dumping.	81.03	5.7.1	✓		Pg. 107		
Develop awareness of acceptable/unacceptable parenting and disciplinary practices. *BEST Plus: Describe whether or not parental involvement in a child's education helps children.*	82.03	3.5.7	✓		Pgs. **112, 113**	Pg. 138	72, 73
Listen and follow directions.	83.01	2.5.4		Pg. 98		Pg. 124	
Paraphrase passages, words, or ideas in conversations.	83.02			Pg. 98	Pgs. 103, **107**, 119	Pg. 126	74
Apply oral communication skills to simple interviews and presentations.	83.04	4.1.5 4.1.7		Pg. 105	Pg. 113	Pgs. 131, 138	
Utilize new vocabulary by context.	83.06			Pgs. 96, 107	Pgs. 104, 113	Pgs. 120, 122, 123, 130, 133, 135, 138, 193, 194	
Recognize sequence of events in a reading passage.	83.07			Pg. 94		Pg. 121	
Preview and make predictions prior to reading.	83.10			Pg. 98	Pgs. 108, 114	Pg. 139	
Interpret statistical information from diagrams, tables, graphs, charts, and schedules.	83.13	6.6.5		Pgs. 96, 97, 110, 111	Pgs. **105**, 120, 121	Pgs. 122, 137	75
Skim and scan to locate information. *BEST Plus: State opinion about the degree to which violence on television may promote violent behavior.*	83.14		✓	Pgs. 96, 97, 100, 104, 109	Pgs. 112, 113, 115	Pgs. 127, 131, 136, 138, 139	
Write a paragraph focusing on one topic (narration, definition, description, cause and effect).	83.15			Pgs. 100, 108, **109**, 110, 111	Pgs. 109, 119, 120, 121	Pgs. 128, 135, 136, 137	76
Write complex and compound sentences with correct terminology and punctuation.	83.16			Pgs. 102, 103	Pgs. 106, 109, 110, **111**, 118	Pgs. 121, 123, 129, 130, 193, 194	77

Unit 6 (continued)

DESCRIPTOR	LCP	CASAS	BEST+	SB	WB	TE	SG
Demonstrate ability to apply a variety of test–taking strategies (multiple choice, true/false, cloze, short essays).	83.18	7.4.7		Pgs. 106, 107	Pgs. 116, 117	Pg. 133	
Use verbs: modals.	84.01		✓			Pg. 127	
Identify parts of speech and use in sentences.	84.02			Pg. 103	Pg. 111	Pg. 129	
Use stress and intonation in phrases and sentences.	85.01		✓	Pg. 105		Pg. 131	

Unit 7: Career Paths

DESCRIPTOR	LCP	CASAS	BEST+	SB	WB	TE	SG
Describe personal career goals, interests, and review jobs including LPN, typist.	69.01	4.1.4 4.1.8 4.4.5 7.1.1			Pgs. 132, **133**, 134, 135	Pgs. 153, 160, 161	78
Use a variety of resources to search for job opportunities and discuss required training.	69.02	4.1.3 4.1.4 4.4.5		Pgs. 114, 115	Pg. 137	Pgs. 143, 153	
Complete job applications and write a résumé and cover letter.	69.03	4.1.2		Pgs. 116, 117, **191**		Pg. 145	79
Demonstrate standards of behavior for job interview; ask and answer questions during a job interview; write a thank you note; conduct a follow-up call after a simulated job interview. *BEST Plus: Describe emotions or feelings about interviews.*	69.04	4.1.5 4.4.1 4.4.3 4.6.2	✓	Pgs. **116**, 124	Pgs. 126, 127, 137	Pgs. 145, 146, 147, 148, 155	80
Demonstrate understanding of job specifications, policies, standards, benefits, W2 and W4 forms. Complete sample W4 form; wages, deductions, and timekeeping forms.	69.05	4.1.1 4.2.1 4.2.3 4.4.4		Pgs. 122, **123**	Pgs. 124, 125	Pgs. 153, 154	81
Demonstrate understanding of U.S. work ethic (appropriate behavior, attire, attitudes, and social interactions that affect job performance).	70.01	4.2.4 4.4.1 4.4.6	✓	Pgs. **112**, 113, 118, 124	Pgs. 122, 123, 124, 128, 129	Pgs. 141, 142, 148, 149, 150, 155, 156, 195	82
Demonstrate basic problem–solving skills in the workplace.	70.02	7.3.4		Pgs. 112, 113	Pgs. 123, 124	Pgs. 142, 152, 196	
Compare and contrast job tasks, responsibilities, and levels of training.	70.03	7.2.3		Pgs. 114, 115	Pgs. 125, **136**	Pg. 143	83
Identify OSHA safety procedures at work.	70.05					Pgs. 195, 196	
Explore options regarding on-the-job opportunities and continuing education to acquire higher-level skills and promotions.	71.01	4.4.2 4.4.4		Pgs. 122, 123	Pgs. 134, 135	Pgs. 153, 161	

Legend:
SB = Student Book   **WB** = Workbook   **TE** = Teacher's Edition   **SG** = Study Guide   **LCP** = Literacy Completion Point
CASAS = Comprehensive Adult Student Assessment System   **BEST+** = Basic English Skills Test, Updated

Correlation Chart

Unit 7 (continued)

DESCRIPTOR	LCP	CASAS	BEST+	SB	WB	TE	SG
Demonstrate an understanding of work performance evaluations and their impact on promotions.	71.02			Pgs. **118**, 119	Pgs. 128, 129	Pgs. 152, 157, 196	84
Demonstrate knowledge of operating equipment necessary for home and work.	72.01				Pgs. 133, 135	Pgs. 143, 147, 149, 153, 160, 161	
Demonstrate ability to take and report accurate messages.	74.01	2.1.7		Pg. 116		Pg. 146	
Read and discuss information related to current events.	80.05	2.6.2 2.7.6 6.8.1			Pgs. 130, 132	Pg. 160	
Identify means to access educational opportunities for children (special programs, scholarships, extracurricular activities).	82.02	2.5.5			Pg. 133	Pg. 160	
Paraphrase passages, words, or ideas in conversations.	83.02				Pg. **139**	Pgs. 152, 196	85
Apply oral communication skills to simple interviews and presentations.	83.04	4.1.5 4.1.7		Pg. 116	Pgs. 126, 127, 135	Pgs. 147, 153, 154, 156, 160, 161	
Utilize new vocabulary by context.	83.06			Pgs. 114, 115, 125	Pg. **123**	Pgs. 143, 156	86
Recognize sequence of events in a reading passage.	83.07			Pgs. **126**, 127	Pgs. 138, 139	Pgs. 158, 159	87
Preview and make predictions prior to reading.	83.10				Pg. 134		
Interpret statistical information from diagrams, tables, graphs, charts, and schedules.	83.13	6.6.5		Pgs. 118, 119, 128	Pgs. 125, 130, **132**, **133**, 134	Pgs. 149, 154, 158, 159, 160	88, 89
Skim and scan to locate information.	83.14				Pgs. 133, 140	Pgs. 150, 160, 195	
Write a paragraph focusing on one topic (narration, definition, description, cause and effect).	83.15			Pgs. 114, 126, 128, 129	Pgs. 139, 141	Pgs. 144, 158, 159	
Write complex and compound sentences with correct terminology and punctuation.	83.16			Pgs. 120, **121**		Pg. 151	90
Read a biography.	83.17			Pg. 127			

Unit 7 (continued)

DESCRIPTOR	LCP	CASAS	BEST+	SB	WB	TE	SG
Demonstrate ability to apply a variety of test–taking strategies (multiple choice, true/false, cloze, short essays).	83.18	7.4.7		Pgs. 124, 125	Pgs. 136, 137	Pgs. 155, 156	
Use verbs: past continuous, past perfect.	84.01		✓	Pgs. 120, 121	Pgs. 130, 131	Pgs. 151, 152, 196	
Identify parts of speech and use in sentences.	84.02				Pg. 124		
Use stress and intonation in phrases and sentences.	85.01		✓			Pg. 144	

Unit 8: Money Matters

DESCRIPTOR	LCP	CASAS	BEST+	SB	WB	TE	SG
Demonstrate understanding of job specifications, policies, standards, benefits, W2 and W4 forms. Complete sample W4 form; wages, deductions, and timekeeping forms.	69.05	4.1.1 4.2.1 4.2.3 4.4.4		Pgs. **140, 141**		Pg. 173	91, 92
Demonstrate knowledge of operating equipment necessary for home and work.	72.01				Pgs. 153, 155	Pgs. 170, 178, 180, 181	
Demonstrate ability to take and report accurate messages.	74.01	2.1.7		Pg. 134		Pgs. 167, 168, 245, 247	
Demonstrate understanding of banking system (loans, interest rates, investments, mortgages), terms, foreign currencies, and exchange rates. *BEST Plus: State opinion about how banks encourage credit card use. State opinion about use of credit cards.*	76.01	1.8.1 1.8.2 1.8.4	✓	Pgs. 132, 133, **134, 135, 142**	Pgs. 144, 145, 146, 147, 156	Pgs. 165, 166, 167, 175, 247	93, 94
Identify budget-planning strategies.	76.02	1.5.1 1.5.2 4.7.1		Pgs. 130, 131, 132, 133	Pgs. **142,** 143, 152, 153	Pgs. 163, 164, 165, 166, 169, 172, 177, 180, 197, 198	95
Identify ways of preventing common crimes (i.e. rape, burglary, domestic assault, car theft, etc.).	78.02	1.6.2 3.4.2 3.5.9 5.3.7 5.3.8	✓	Pgs. 136, 137	Pgs. **148, 149**	Pgs. 166, 170	96, 97
Compare/contrast advertisements, labels, and charts to select goods and services.	79.03	1.2.1 1.3.1 1.3.5 1.6.1		Pgs. 134, 135	Pgs. 146, 147	Pg. 169	
Read and discuss information related to current events.	80.05	2.6.2 2.7.6 6.8.1			Pgs. 154, **155,** 157, 158, 159	Pg. 181	98

Legend:
SB = Student Book   WB = Workbook   TE = Teacher's Edition   SG = Study Guide   LCP = Literacy Completion Point
CASAS = Comprehensive Adult Student Assessment System   BEST+ = Basic English Skills Test, Updated

Correlation Chart

Unit 8 (continued)

DESCRIPTOR	LCP	CASAS	BEST+	SB	WB	TE	SG
Develop awareness of acceptable/unacceptable parenting and disciplinary practices.	82.03	3.5.7			Pgs. **152, 153**	Pg. 180	99, 100
Paraphrase passages, words, or ideas in conversations.	83.02			Pg. 139	Pgs. 150, 151	Pgs. 171, 198	
Apply oral communication skills to simple interviews and presentations.	83.04	4.1.5 4.1.7		Pgs. 134, 136, 138		Pgs. 169, 170, 173, 176, 178, 180	
Utilize new vocabulary by context.	83.06			Pgs. 132, 133, 143	Pgs. 143, **144**, 148, 153	Pgs. 165, 176, 180, 246, 248	101
Preview and make predictions prior to reading.	83.10			Pgs. 144, 145	Pgs. 154, **158**	Pgs. 178, 181	102
Interpret statistical information from diagrams, tables, graphs, charts, and schedules.	83.13	6.6.5		Pgs. 135, 144	Pgs. 142, 145, 147, **154, 155,** 157	Pgs. 170, 178, 181	103
Skim and scan to locate information.	83.14			Pgs. 140, 144, 145		Pgs. 166, 173, 178, 197	
Write a paragraph focusing on one topic (narration, definition, description, cause and effect).	83.15			Pgs. 128, 129, 147	Pgs. 149, 161	Pg. 179	
Write complex and compound sentences with correct terminology and punctuation.	83.16			Pg. 138	Pgs. 144, 150, 151, 159	Pgs. 171, 172, 174, 198	
Demonstrate ability to apply a variety of test–taking strategies (multiple choice, true/false, cloze, short essays).	83.18	7.4.7		Pgs. 142, 143	Pgs. 156, 157	Pgs. 175, 176	
Identify parts of speech and use in sentences.	84.02			Pgs. 146, 147	Pg. 143	Pg. 179	

Legend:
SB = Student Book   WB = Workbook   TE = Teacher's Edition   SG = Study Guide   LCP = Literacy Completion Point
CASAS = Comprehensive Adult Student Assessment System   BEST+ = Basic English Skills Test, Updated

All-Star 4 Study Guide

Student Name _____   Date _____

Instructor Name _____

---

2 Read the article and answer the questions below with facts from the article.

With Big Risks Come Big Rewards for Immigrant Family
by Christina Lima

In 1979, To and Hong Trieu arrived in Portland, Oregon from war-ravaged Vietnam. To was 30 and Hong was 22. Once in the United States, they married and dreamed of having children and getting good jobs. But finding work wasn't easy. They spoke little English, so their choices were limited to jobs such as washing dishes and cleaning floors.

Now, many years later, things have **turned around** for the Trieus. They own two successful Asian restaurants. "It's a dream come true. I feel **fulfilled**," Hong Trieu says. The Trieus' story reveals a sharp business sense. The couple blends Vietnamese and Chinese cuisines to reflect their Vietnamese birthplace and Chinese ancestry, and to capture a larger market. They've picked busy locations for their restaurants. And, perhaps more than anything, they've listened closely to their customers, many of whom insisted they expand both the dining space and the restaurants' hours.

Source: www.oregonlive.com

1. How long ago did To and Hong come to the United States?

   _____

2. What goals did they have when they came to the United States?

   _____

3. Why did they have trouble finding good jobs when they first came to the United States?

   _____

4. What do the Trieus do for work now?

   _____

5. What did their customers want them to do?

   _____

3 Give an inference about the Trieus based on the factual information below.

1. To and Hong didn't speak much English when they came to the U.S.
   To and Hong probably didn't study English for very long in Vietnam.

2. To and Hong own two successful Asian restaurants.

   _____

3. It was difficult for the Trieus to find work when they came to the U.S.

   _____

4. To and Hong listened to their customers and expanded the size of the dining area.

   _____

5. The Trieus have lived in the U.S. since 1979.

   _____

Describe personal career goals, interests, and review jobs including LPN, typist. *BEST Plus:* Identify self and share personal information about country of origin and current residence. Discuss learning new skills and interests. Describe learning goals and best ways to learn new things. Student Book page 19. LCP- E 69.01 . . . CASAS 4.1.4, 4.1.8, 4.4.5, 7.1.1 . . . BEST *Plus*

BEST *Plus:* How long have you lived in the U.S.? Where is your family from? What are the qualities of a good learner? What new things would you like to learn? What can you do to improve your English?

All-Star 4 Study Guide

Student Name _____   **Date** _____

Instructor Name _____

See Student Book page 20. Label the parts of Letter B.

Demonstrate standards of behavior for job interview; ask and answer questions during a job interview; write a thank you note; conduct a follow-up call after a simulated job interview. *BEST Plus: Discuss emotional state of being about job interviews.* Student Book page 21. LCP-E 69.04 … CASAS 4.1.5, 4.4.1, 4.4.3, 4.6.2 … BEST *Plus*

Letter B: Full-block Style

_____

4355 Bryson Avenue
Chicago, IL 60607
November 14, 2005

_____

Ms. Anna Phillio
Director, Customer Service
Real Goods Company
4335 West Wilson Avenue
Chicago, IL 60625

_____

Dear Ms. Phillio,

_____

Thank you for the opportunity to interview for a position as sales associate. Talking with you yesterday strengthened my interest in working for Real Goods. I believe that with my educational and work background, I could carry out the responsibilities of a sales associate with both energy and confidence. I look forward to hearing from you.

_____

Sincerely,

Daisy Miller

_____

Daisy Miller

2 How is the semi-block style different from the full-block style? List 2 things.

> EXAMPLE: The semi-block style has the heading in the upper right while the full-block style has the heading in the upper left.

_____

_____

3 Write a sample business letter to the Speedy English Language Program. Imagine that you want to take classes. Ask for specific information about their program. Use either the semi-block style or the full-block style for your business letter. Address your letter to:

Howard Smith, Director
Speedy English Language Program
1234 16th Street NW
Washington, DC 20036

BEST *Plus:* Do you get nervous during a job interview?

All-Star 4 Study Guide

Student Name _____   Date _____

Instructor Name _____

See Student Book pages 8–9.

Demonstrate ability to take and report accurate messages. Student Book page 8. LCP-E 74.01 . . . CASAS 2.1.7

THINGS TO DO

1 Warm Up

Work with your classmates to answer these questions.

1. Do you have a telephone answering machine or service? What does the message say?
2. Read the list of Telephone Do's and Don'ts. Add two more ideas to each list.

2 Listen for General Information 🎧

Listen to 6 telephone calls and number them in order from first (1) to last (6).

___ Someone calls to inquire about a job.
___ Someone calls to apologize for something.
_1_ Someone calls to ask a favor.
___ The caller hears a message about business hours.
___ Someone calls to invite someone to something.
___ The caller is returning a call.

3 Listen for Specific Information 🎧

Read the telephone messages on page 9 and listen to the 6 telephone calls again. Add the missing information to the messages.

4 Use the Communication Strategy 🎧

Choose a reason for calling a classmate. Practice leaving a message on his or her answering machine. Then ask your classmates to evaluate your message. Use the communication strategy on this page.

A: You have reached the Li family. Please leave a message.

B: Hi. This is Rick Martinez calling for Jim. Jim, I'm calling to get the homework assignment for English class. Could you please call me at 555-8933? Thanks. Bye.

All-Star 4 Study Guide

Student Name _____ Date _____

Instructor Name _____

A For each category below, add 2 more examples.

Category	Examples
1) Ways parents can be involved in their children's education	• they can volunteer at school • •
2) Ways parents can discipline their children	• they can take something away • •
3) Way parents can encourage their children to read	• they can praise them • •

B Read the article below. How important do you think it is for parents to do each thing? Write *VI (very important), SI (somewhat important),* or *NI (not important)* on the lines.

Eight Things Teachers Wish Parents Would Do
Brought to you by the National PTA®

1. **Be involved.** Parent involvement helps students learn, improves schools, and helps teachers work with you to help your children succeed. _____

2. **Provide resources at home for learning.** Use your local library, and have books and magazines available in your home. Read with your children each day. _____

3. **Set a good example.** Show your children by your own actions that you believe reading is both enjoyable and useful. Monitor[1] television viewing. _____

4. **Encourage students to do their best in school.** Show your children that you believe education is important and that you want them to do their best. _____

5. **Value education and seek a balance[2] between schoolwork and outside activities.** Emphasize[3] your children's progress in developing the knowledge and skills they need to be successful both in school and in life. _____

6. **Support school rules and goals.** Take care not to undermine[4] school rules, discipline, or goals. _____

7. **Use pressure[5] positively.** Encourage children to do their best, but don't pressure them by setting goals too high or by scheduling too many activities. _____

8. **Call teachers early if you think there's a problem.** Call while there is still time to solve the problem. Don't wait for teachers to call you. _____

[1]monitor: observe, watch over
[2]balance: not too much of one or the other
[3]emphasize: place importance on

[4]undermine: ruin the efforts of
[5]pressure: the making of demands

Excerpted from "Top Ten Things Teachers Wish Parents Would Do" from www.familyeducation.com. Used with permission from National PTA, www.pta.org.

All-Star 4 Study Guide

Student Name _____   Date _____

Instructor Name _____

Apply oral communication skills to simple interviews and presentations. Student Book page 14. LCP-E 83.04 . . . CASAS 4.1.5, 4.1.7

1 Warm Up

Work with your classmates to answer the questions below.

1. Have you ever had a job interview? What questions did the interviewer ask you?
2. What advice would you give someone who was going to a job interview?

2 Read and Respond

Read this article and complete the chart below. Then compare charts with your classmates.

Job Interview Questions

When you interview for a job, the interviewer is very likely to ask about your skills and abilities. Below are three common questions that interviewers ask:

1. Tell me about yourself.

This is a very general request and it can be difficult to know what to say and what not to say. Basically, the interviewer wants a quick **overview** of your work and educational background with a focus on your accomplishments. The interviewer is not interested in learning about your personal life or your personal problems. He or she wants to know about your skills and abilities. Don't be afraid to use strong adjectives such as dependable, creative, cooperative, competent, and determined to describe yourself.

2. What is your greatest strength?

You might be a very creative cook for your friends or an **incredibly** patient parent, but the interviewer probably doesn't want to hear about your strengths at home. Instead, identify one of your strengths and explain how it could be useful in a work situation. A creative cook might say that she enjoys coming up with new ways to do things. She should give an example showing how she's done that in a work environment. A patient parent could say that he is a good listener who likes to work with others to resolve problems.

3. What is your greatest weakness?

When you answer this question, focus on the positive not the negative. Identify a work-related weakness that could be viewed as a strength, and then immediately tell what you did or are now doing to **overcome** this weakness. For example, you might say that when you see a problem, you feel a responsibility to solve it. As a result, you sometimes have more to do than you can handle. You are resolving that by learning to distribute work more equally.

Interview Question	Do's	Don'ts
Tell me about yourself.	give a summary of your work and school background.	
What is your greatest strength?		
What is your greatest weakness?		

All-Star 4 Study Guide

Student Name _____   Date _____

Instructor Name _____

MAKING INFERENCES

A fact is information that can be verified, or shown to be true. An inference is a logical conclusion based on factual information. An inference is an interpretation of a fact.

EXAMPLES:

Fact:	Oscar found the problem with my computer and fixed it.
Inference:	Oscar is a good problem solver.
Fact:	Oscar always gets to work on time.
Inference:	Oscar is dependable.

When you read, it's important to distinguish facts from inferences. It's also important to be able to make logical inferences from the facts you read.

1 Read each fact below. Then check (✓) the logical inference in each pair.

1. **Fact:** Everyone in the class failed the test.

   Inferences: ☐ The test was very difficult.

   ☐ Everyone in the class understood the material.

2. **Fact:** It's about 200 miles from Boston to New York.

   Inferences: ☐ You can't fly from Boston to New York.

   ☐ It takes about 4 hours to drive from Boston to New York.

3. **Fact:** Carlos spoke Spanish to his grandmother.

   Inferences: ☐ Carlos is bilingual.

   ☐ Carlos's grandmother understands Spanish.

4. **Fact:** Taka wants to take a computer course.

   Inferences: ☐ Taka has excellent computer skills.

   ☐ Taka wants to improve her computer skills.

5. **Fact:** Manuel stopped talking on his cell phone when he realized it disturbed his coworkers.

   Inferences: ☐ Manuel has good interpersonal skills.

   ☐ Manuel doesn't like to talk on the telephone.

All-Star 4 Study Guide

Student Name _____   **Date** _____

Instructor Name _____

See Student Book page 11.

THINGS TO DO

1 Warm Up

Work with your classmates to answer the questions below.

1. In what jobs is it important to have good writing skills?
2. In your personal life, when is it useful to have good writing skills?
3. Skim, or read quickly, the article on page 11 to find the main ideas or facts. Then complete the chart below.

> Title of the Article: _____
>
> Source (where it is from): _____
>
> Topic (what it is about): _____

2 Read and Respond

Read the article on page 11 and answer these questions below.

1. According to the article, what do 33% of employees fail at?
2. Who is Susan Traiman and why does the writer **quote** her?
3. Why are writing skills more important today than 20 years ago?
4. According to the article, why is it a good idea to improve your writing skills?
5. Of the six writing problems listed in the article, which is the most difficult for you? Why?

3 Evaluate

Read the email messages on page 11 and answer the questions below. Write *yes* or *no*. Circle the mistakes and underline the unclear portions. Then correct the mistakes.

	Email #1	Email #2
1. Are there any spelling mistakes?	_____	_____
2. Is there any missing punctuation?	_____	_____
3. Are there any grammar mistakes?	_____	_____
4. Is it clear?	_____	_____
5. Is it concise?	_____	_____

Skim and scan to locate information. Student Book page 10. LCP-E 83.14

All-Star 4 Study Guide

Student Name _____   Date _____

Instructor Name _____

DIRECTIONS: Read the business letter below to answer the next 4 questions. Use the Answer Sheet.

122 Fifth St., Apt. 5B
San Aremo, CA 92456

January 10, 2005

Product Safety Department
Just 4 Fun Toys
155 Highway 11
Darby, NJ 07059

To Whom It May Concern:

On December 23rd, I purchased a Rolling Rover toy at your store in San José, California. Soon after I gave it to my two-year-old son, one of the small wheels came off. Since these wheels are small enough for a child to swallow, I am very concerned that this toy could cause injury to another child.

I urge you to correct this problem quickly so that no children are harmed in the future.

Yours truly,

Geneva Spring
Geneva Spring

ANSWER SHEET

1 (A) (B) (C) (D)
2 (A) (B) (C) (D)
3 (A) (B) (C) (D)
4 (A) (B) (C) (D)
5 (A) (B) (C) (D)
6 (A) (B) (C) (D)
7 (A) (B) (C) (D)
8 (A) (B) (C) (D)
9 (A) (B) (C) (D)
10 (A) (B) (C) (D)

1. What was the writer's purpose for writing this letter?

A. to thank someone for something
B. to ask a question
C. to ask for money
D. to report a problem

2. Where is the writer's address?

A. on the upper right side
B. on the upper left side
C. on the lower left side
D. on the lower right side

3. What other salutation could you use for a business letter?

A. Yours truly,
B. Hi
C. Dear Sir / Madam
D. Your friend,

4. Where did the writer sign the letter?

A. below the heading
B. above the closing
C. below the closing
D. above the salutation

All-Star 4 Study Guide

Student Name _____   Date _____

Instructor Name _____

DIRECTIONS: Read the job interview tips to answer the next 6 questions.

JOB INTERVIEW TIPS

1) Leave extra time to get to a job interview. It's important that you arrive a few minutes before the interview is supposed to begin.
2) Make sure your appearance is neat and dress appropriately. It's usually better to be overdressed than underdressed.
3) Try not to appear nervous during the interview. Avoid nervous habits such as chewing gum and playing with things in your hand.
4) Speak clearly and concisely and always tell the truth.
5) Make eye contact with the interviewer and speak confidently.
6) Focus on what you can do for the company. Wait until you have been offered the job to ask about the salary and benefits.
7) Use examples from your work and educational background to show that you are hard working, honest, responsible, and a team player.
8) At the end of the interview, shake hands and thank the interviewer for his or her time. You can also say that you are looking forward to hearing from him or her.

5. According to the article, when should you arrive at a job interview?

A. exactly on time
B. a half hour early
C. a little early
D. a little late

6. According to the article, what is one sign of nervousness?

A. looking around
B. playing with things in your hand
C. making eye contact
D. arriving early

7. Which example would show you are a hard worker?

A. I grew up on a farm.
B. I like to get up early in the morning.
C. In addition to my job, I am taking two evening courses.
D. I think I'm a hard worker.

8. Which of these things shouldn't you do at a job interview?

A. speak clearly
B. look directly at the interviewer
C. ask first about the job benefits
D. dress neatly

9. What could you say to show that you are a team player?

A. I enjoy working on group projects.
B. I have a big family.
C. I like team sports.
D. I like to meet new people.

10. Which sentence would be appropriate for you to say at the end of a job interview?

A. When will I hear from you?
B. I hope you don't interview anyone else.
C. I'll call you tomorrow.
D. Thank you for your time.

Demonstrate ability to apply a variety of test-taking strategies (mulitple choice, true/false, cloze, short essays). Workbook page 17. LCP-E 83.18 . . . . CASAS 7.4.7

All-Star 4 Study Guide

Student Name _____   Date _____

Instructor Name _____

A Add the missing words to the chart and complete the questions below. Then answer the questions.

ADJECTIVES	ADVERBS
1.	essentially
2. clear	
3. concise	
4.	proficiently
5.	responsibly
6.	cooperatively
7. different	
8. good	
9.	possibly
10.	easily

1. What is _____essential_____ for all children to have? _____

2. Was the sky _____ yesterday? _____

3. Is it important to give instructions _____ in an emergency? _____

4. How long does it take to become a _____ driver? _____

5. Who is _____ for cooking in your family? _____

6. Why is it sometimes difficult to work _____? _____

7. How is English _____ from your first language? _____

8. What do you wish you could do _____? _____

9. Is it _____ for an immigrant to become a U.S. senator or representative? _____

10. What sport is _____ to learn how to play? _____

1. _____

2. _____

3. _____

4. _____

5. _____

6. _____

7. _____

8. _____

9. _____

10. _____

All-Star 4 Study Guide

Student Name _____   Date _____

Instructor Name _____

Use consonant blends, dipthongs, and digraphs. Student Book page 15. LCP-E 85.02 . . . BEST *Plus*

WINDOW ON PRONUNCIATION 🎧
Blending Words in Questions with *You*

A Sometimes when two consonants are next to each other we blend the sounds together. Listen to the phrases below. Listen again and repeat.

| can't you | did you | haven't you | shouldn't you |
| could you | don't you | should you | would you |

B Write the phrases from Activity A in the correct column below.

Underlined letters sound like *j* (as in *juice*)	Underlined letters sound like *ch* (as in *chew*)
	can't you

C Listen to the sentences. Write the missing phrases from Activity A. Then take turns with a partner asking and answering the questions.

1. _____ have any supervisory experience in your last position?
2. _____ tell me what your greatest strength is?
3. _____ describe your duties in your last job?
4. _____ like to study something new?

All-Star 4 Study Guide

Student Name _____   Date _____

Instructor Name _____

B Use the highway map to answer the questions below.

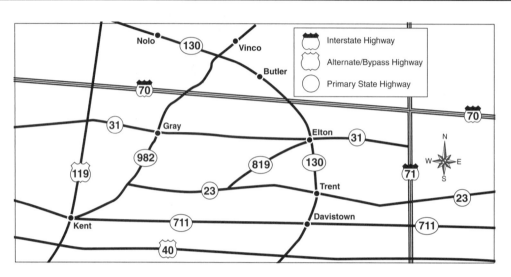

1. According to the map, which interstate highway goes north/south?

   A. Rt. 31   B. Rt. 70   C. Rt. 71   D. Rt. 130

2. Which road runs parallel to Rt. 711?

   A. Rt. 119   B. Rt. 40   C. Rt. 819   D. Rt. 982

3. Which town is directly north of Gray?

   A. Nolo   B. Elton   C. Kent   D. Trent

4. Which is the shortest route from Kent to Elton?

   A. Rt. 711 to 130   B. Rt. 119 to 31   C. Rt. 982 to 23 to 819   D. Rt. 982 to 70 to 130

5. Which road connects Davistown and Trent?

   A. Interstate 71   B. Rt. 119   C. Rt. 130   D. Rt 711

6. Which road is an interstate highway?

   A. 23   B. 71   C. 819   D. 119

C Use the map above to complete these directions. Write *east, west, north,* or *south.*

1. To get from Gray to Elton you should go _____ on Route 31.

2. To get from Elton to Butler, you should go _____ on Route 130.

3. You can take Route 982 _____ to go from Kent to Gray.

4. The shortest way from Trent to Kent is to take 23 _____ and 982
   _____ .

5. To get from Butler to Interstate 71, just go _____ on 130 until you reach Interstate 70.

   Then go _____ on 70 until you hit Interstate 71.

All-Star 4 Study Guide

Student Name _____   Date _____

Instructor Name _____

A Complete the sentences with *should have* or *shouldn't have*.

1. Jamal missed his flight because he got stuck in traffic and was late to the airport. I guess he _____ left home earlier.

2. I didn't see the car behind me and I backed into it. I guess I _____ looked behind more carefully.

3. I felt sick at work all day today. I guess I _____ gone to work. I _____ stayed home.

4. Juan had to pay a lot for his plane ticket because he didn't buy it until two days before the flight. Now he knows he _____ bought it at least two weeks before the flight.

5. The airlines lost Sandra's luggage so for three days she didn't have any clean clothes to wear. Now she knows she _____ put some clothes in her carry-on bag.

6. Ali _____ taken Route 90 because there's always a traffic jam during rush hour.

B Answer the questions below about the world's worst driver.

1. When Tony saw the stop sign, he ignored it. What should he have done?

_____

2. When Tony saw the blinking yellow light, he sped up. What should he have done?

_____

3. When Tony saw the blinking red light, he slowed down a little. What should he have done?

_____

4. When Tony saw pedestrians in the crosswalk, he didn't stop. What should he have done?

_____

5. When Tony heard an ambulance behind him, he didn't move his car over. What should he have done?

_____

Identify and explain common problems and solutions. Workbook page 30. LCP-E 73.02 . . . CASAS 7.3.1, 7.3.2, 7.3.3

All-Star 4 Study Guide

Student Name _____   Date _____

Instructor Name _____

Identify and explain common problems and solutions. Workbook page 31. LCP-E 73.02 . . . CASAS 7.3.1, 7.3.2, 7.3.3

C Study the photographs and answer the questions.

1. Samantha got ketchup on her white shirt. What could she have done to avoid this? List 3 things.

   - *She could have* _____

     _____

   - _____

     _____

   - _____

     _____

2. What do you think she should have done?

   _____

   _____

3. Chan got wet while he was waiting for the bus to arrive. What could he have done to avoid this? List 3 things.

   - _____

   - _____

   - _____

4. What do you think he should have done?

   _____

   _____

All-Star 4 Study Guide for Post-Testing Copyright © McGraw-Hill

All-Star 4 Study Guide

Student Name _____   Date _____

Instructor Name _____

See Student Book page 25.

---

2 Read and Respond

Do you know what to do if you are in a car accident? Read the information below and answer the questions. Then fill in the missing information about Tom Rideout's accident. See page 25 for his insurance information.

Car Accident Checklist

- Stop immediately. Keep calm. Do not argue, accuse anyone, or make any admission of guilt for the accident.
- Do not leave the scene; however, if the vehicles are operable, move them to the **shoulder of the road** and out of the way of **oncoming** traffic.
- **Warn** oncoming traffic.
- Call medical assistance for anyone injured. Dial 911. Do what you can to provide first aid, but do not move them unless you know what you are doing.
- Call appropriate law enforcement authorities.
- Get the information requested in the form below.

Other Vehicle Information

Owner: _Thomas Rideout_   Phone: _(305) 555-3465_

Address: _____

Make/Model/Year: _____

Vehicle ID: _____

License Plate #/State: _883WE / Florida_

Driver's Name: _____

Phone: _(305) 555-3465_

Address: _564 Philips St. Miami, FL 33136_

Driver's License #/State: _FLD000590 / Florida_

Area of Damage: _bumper, windshield, headlights_

Accident Facts

Date: _Nov. 6_   Time: _8:45 AM_

City, State/Street: _Miami, FL / Route 41_

Condition of Road/Weather: _dry / clear and sunny_

Direction of your Car: _west_

Speed of your Car: _I was stopped._

Direction of other Car: _west_

Speed of other Car: _About 25 mph. Ran into backend_

Did the police take a report? _Yes._

Responding Police Department: _Florida Highway Patrol_

Case/Report Number: _FL2222XYZ_

Witnesses

Name: _Han Chen_   Phone: _(813) 555-1263_

Address: _1275 75 St. Tampa, FL 33619_

Name: _N/A_   Phone: _____

Address: _____

Source: AAA Insurance, http://www.ouraaa.com

QUESTIONS

1. According to the car accident checklist, what are 3 things you should do if you are in an accident? What are 3 things you shouldn't do?
2. In a serious accident, which would you do first—call 911 or move your car onto the shoulder of the road? Why?
3. How could you warn oncoming traffic that there has been an accident?
4. Why shouldn't you move an injured person?
5. Why is it important to get the names of any witnesses?

Follow emergency procedures and complete medical forms and accident reports. Student Book pages 32–33. LCP-E 75.02 . . . CASAS 3.2.1

All-Star 4 Study Guide

Student Name _____ **Date** _____

Instructor Name _____

See Student Book page 29.

Compare/contrast basic factors when planning a trip (distance, cost, tips, comfort and convenience). *BEST Plus: Describe how you choose a method of transportation.* Student Book page 28. LCP-E 77.01 … CASAS 1.1.3, 1.2.2, 1.9.3, 1.9.4, 2.2.4, 2.2.5, 2.6.3 … *BEST Plus*

2 Read and Compare

Read the email on page 29 and take notes in the chart below. Then add your own ideas under "Other Expenses."

Travel Options	Travel Time	Cost of Ticket (Round Trip)	Other Expenses
Plane		$300.00	• *bus to airport* • *$100.00 to change ticket*
Bus			
Train			
Car			

Compare charts with a classmate and answer the questions below.

1. What's the fastest way for Jackie to get to California? What's the slowest way?
2. What are the advantages of traveling by train? What are the disadvantages?
3. If Jackie decides to travel across the country by car, what expenses would she have in addition to gasoline?
4. If Jackie travels by train, what cities will she go through?
5. How does Jackie plan to get to California?

1. _____

2. _____

3. _____

4. _____

5. _____

BEST *Plus:* How do you decide on a method of transportation?

All-Star 4 Study Guide

Student Name _____ Date _____

Instructor Name _____

Complete the sample test.

Department of Motor Vehicles, California
Sample Driver Test

1. You may drive off of the paved roadway to pass another vehicle:

   ○ If the shoulder is wide enough to accommodate your vehicle.
   ○ If the vehicle ahead of you is turning left.
   ○ Under no circumstances.

2. You are approaching a railroad crossing with no warning devices and are unable to see 400 feet down the tracks in one direction. The speed limit is:

   ○ 15 mph
   ○ 20 mph
   ○ 25 mph

3. When parking your vehicle parallel to the curb on a level street:

   ○ Your front wheels must be turned toward the street.
   ○ Your wheels must be within 18 inches of the curb.
   ○ One of your rear wheels must touch the curb.

4. When you are merging onto the freeway, you should be driving:

   ○ At or near the same speed as the traffic on the freeway.
   ○ 5 to 10 MPH slower than the traffic on the freeway.
   ○ The posted speed limit for traffic on the freeway.

5. When driving in fog, you should use your:

   ○ Fog lights only.
   ○ High beams.
   ○ Low beams.

6. A white painted curb means:

   ○ Loading zone for freight or passengers.
   ○ Loading zone for passengers or mail only.
   ○ Loading zone for freight only.

7. A school bus ahead of you in your lane is stopped with red lights flashing. You should:

   ○ Stop, then proceed when you think all of the children have exited the bus.
   ○ Slow to 25 MPH and pass cautiously.
   ○ Stop as long as the red lights are flashing.

8. California's "Basic Speed Law" says:

   ○ You should never drive faster than posted speed limits.
   ○ You should never drive faster than is safe for current conditions.
   ○ The maximum speed limit in California is 70 mph on certain freeways.

9. You just sold your vehicle. You must notify the DMV within ___ days.

   ○ 5
   ○ 10
   ○ 15

10. To avoid last minute moves, you should be looking down the road to where your vehicle will be in about _____.

    ○ 5 to 10 seconds
    ○ 10 to 15 seconds
    ○ 15 to 20 seconds

Answers:

1. Under no circumstances.
2. 15 mph
3. Your wheels must be within 18 inches of the curb.
4. At or near the same speed as the traffic on the freeway.
5. Low beams.
6. Loading zone for passengers or mail only.
7. Stop as long as the red lights are flashing.
8. You should never drive faster than is safe for current conditions.
9. 5
10. 10 to 15 seconds

Source: http://www.dmv.ca.gov.

Discuss U.S. driving responsibilities and driver's license exam with emphasis on auto insurance (driver's license, traffic regulations, insurance, seat belts, child safety restraints). *BEST Plus: Describe driving/seatbelt safety and safety of children.* Student Book page 188. LCP-E 77.02 ... CASAS 1.9.1, 1.9.2, 1.9.8, 2.2.1, 2.2.2 ...BEST Plus

BEST *Plus:* Do you always wear a seatbelt?

All-Star 4 Study Guide

Student Name _____   **Date** _____

Instructor Name _____

See Student Book page 25.

See Student Book page 25.

THINGS TO DO

1 Talk about It

Use the *Dictionary of Common Automobile Insurance Terms* on this page to answer these questions.

1. Which terms in the list do you know?
2. Is it important to have collision insurance? Why or why not?
3. What is the difference between collision and comprehensive coverage?

2 Write *True* or *False*

Study the insurance **policy** on page 25 and read the statements below. For each statement, write *True* or *False*.

1. The name of the policyholder is Thomas Rideout.   _____
2. The policy holder owns a Toyota.   _____
3. The policy holder drives about 10,000 miles a year.   _____
4. His insurance policy is good for 6 months.   _____
5. Tom pays $50,000.00 for his liability coverage.   _____
6. Tom got a discount on his insurance policy because he is a good driver.   _____
7. Tom has a $500.00 deductible.   _____
8. Tom's bill for car insurance comes to $256.80.   _____
9. Tom has an alarm system in his car.   _____
10. The insurance company is in Florida.   _____

Now correct the false statements.

3 Apply

Read each situation below and answer the question. Then compare ideas with your classmates.

1. Someone stole your car and the police never found it. Which coverage would pay for your loss?
2. A rock from a passing truck cracked your windshield. Which coverage would cover your loss?
3. You haven't had a car accident in 7 years. Do you think you can get a discount on your insurance?

Dictionary of Common Automobile Insurance Terms

1. **Actual Cash Value** The cost to replace a vehicle minus the amount it has **depreciated** since you bought it.
2. **Bodily Injury Liability** This covers medical expenses for injuries the **policyholder** causes to someone else.
3. **Claim** The policyholder's request for **reimbursement** of a loss covered by their insurance policy.
4. **Collision** This covers damage to the policyholder's car from any collision. The collision could be with another car, a wall, a rock, etc.
5. **Comprehensive** This covers damage to the policyholder's car from something other than another car, such as theft, fire, or earthquake.
6. **Deductible** The part of the loss that you agree to pay if you have an accident.
7. **Medical Payments or Personal Injury Protection (PIP)** This covers the treatment of injuries to the driver and passengers of the policyholder's **vehicle**.
8. **Premium** The amount of money you pay for your insurance. The higher the deductible, the lower the premium.
9. **Property Damage Liability** This pays for damage the policyholder causes to someone else's property.
10. **Uninsured Motorist Coverage** This pays for treatment and/or property damages of the policyholder if he/she is injured in a collision with an uninsured driver.

Compare/contrast various types of insurance policies (life, health, homeowner's, renter's, vehicle). Student Book page 24. LCP-E 79.04 . . . CASAS 1.4.6, 1.9.8, 3.2.3

All-Star 4 Study Guide

Student Name _____   Date _____

Instructor Name _____

A Read each paragraph below and identify the topic and the main idea.

1

The last trip I took was in 2003. That year I went to Italy to visit my brother. I thought this would be a great trip, but in fact, it was pretty awful. The worst thing that happened was that my brother got the flu and he had to stay in bed the whole time I was there. Besides that, the airlines lost my luggage on the flight over so for the first three days of my trip, I didn't have any clean clothes to put on. And then, to top it off, it rained every day I was there.

Topic: _____

Main Idea: _____

_____

_____

2

Yesterday a car pulled into the road right in front of me. The driver was talking on his cell phone and he never even saw me. It was only because I stepped on the brake that I was able to avoid an accident. Another time I was driving on the highway and a car passed me going quite fast. When I looked at the driver, I noticed that he was shaving his face! It's amazing the stupid things people will do while they are driving.

Topic: _____

Main Idea: _____

_____

_____

_____

3

There are many different ways to get around in the United States. Many cities have buses, trains (or "subways"), trolleys, or streetcars. For a small fee, you can ride these vehicles. In some places, you can buy a card good for several trips on subways or buses. You can also pay for each trip separately. Taxicabs, or "taxis," are cars that take you where you want to go for a fee. Taxis are more expensive than other types of public transportation.

Topic: _____

Main Idea: _____

_____

_____

_____

4

Owning a car is a convenient way to get around but it's expensive too. In addition to paying for the car, you have to pay for car insurance and registration. You also have to pay for car maintenance and repairs. And don't forget the cost of gasoline, parking, and tolls. It's important to think of all the costs before you decide to buy a car.

Topic: _____

Main Idea: _____

_____

_____

Comprehend selected reading passages recognizing the main idea. Workbook page 38. LCP-E 83.05

All-Star 4 Study Guide

Student Name _____   Date _____

Instructor Name _____

Write complex and compound sentences with correct terminology and punctuation. Student Book page 39. LCP-E 83.16

WRITING COMPOUND SENTENCES

A compound sentence consists of two or more simple sentences joined by a coordinating conjunction (*and, but, or*) or by a semicolon (;) if a coordinating conjunction is not used.

EXAMPLES:

Traveling by plane can be inexpensive, **but** you may need to spend a lot of time looking for a cheap fare.

Even numbered interstates run east-west; odd numbered interstates run north-south.

---

2 Join each pair of sentences below to make compound sentences.

1. Hitchhiking is not common in the United States.

   In many parts of the country, hitchhiking is illegal.

   _____

2. Taxis are more expensive than most other kinds of public transportation.

   Taxis take you exactly where you want to go.

   _____

3. In some states, you can make a right turn at a red light.

   Before you make a right turn at a red light, you must come to a complete stop.

   _____

4. Each state has different rules for getting a driver's license.

   All states require you to take a driving test.

   _____

5. Driving across the country takes a lot of time.
   Driving across the country allows you to see more than if you fly.

   _____

All-Star 4 Study Guide

Student Name _____   Date _____

Instructor Name _____

Use verbs: past continuous, past perfect, modals, conditionals, gerunds, participles, infinitives.
Student Book page 31. LCP-E 84.01 . . . BEST *Plus*

The Past Form of *Could*

You can use *could (not) have* + a past participle to identify something that was possible (or impossible) in the past. This structure is used to talk about an option not taken.

EXAMPLES:

I **could have left** on Monday, but I decided to wait until Tuesday.
Jude **could have bought** a new car, but he decided to buy a used car.
You **couldn't have booked** a ticket because your name is not on the flight list.

I You He/She/It We They	**could have taken** the train instead of the bus. **could have gotten** a cheaper fare by booking early. **couldn't have seen** the accident because it was too dark.

3 Write

Answer each question with a complete sentence.

1. Ann rented a car to travel from Miami, Florida to New York. How else could she have traveled to New York?

   She could have flown.

2. Mohamed used a credit card to buy his plane ticket. How else could he have bought his ticket?

   _____

3. Fatima only bought liability insurance for her car. What other kind of coverage could she have bought?

   _____

4. Andrea left her computer in the car and someone stole it. What could she have done to avoid losing her computer?

   _____

5. Ray was late to the meeting because he got caught in rush hour traffic. How could he have avoided being late?

   _____

6. Tranh tried to stop his car, but the streets were wet and he crashed into the car in front of him. What could Tranh have done (or not done) in this situation?

   _____

7. Marcos bought his plane ticket from a travel agent. Where else could he have bought his ticket?

   _____

All-Star 4 Study Guide

Student Name _____   Date _____

Instructor Name _____

Use consonant blends, dipthongs, and digraphs. Student Book page 33. LCP-E 85.02 . . . BEST *Plus*

WINDOW ON PRONUNCIATION 🎧
Reduction of Past Modals

A Listen to the words. Then listen and repeat.

should have (sounds like *shuduv*)   shouldn't have (sounds like *shudnuv*)
could have (sounds like *cuduv*)   couldn't have (sounds like *cudnuv*)

B Listen to the sentences. Write the missing words. Use the correct spelling.

1. I _____ renewed my driver's license earlier this month.

2. He _____ taken an earlier flight.

3. They _____ chosen a worse time to travel.

4. She _____ slowed down at the intersection.

5. You _____ purchased insurance from that company.

6. We _____ bought our tickets online.

C Work with a partner. Ask the questions below. Write your partner's answers.

1. Think about the last trip you took. What are two things you should have done differently?

_____

2. What could you have done to help someone last week?
   What did you do to help someone last week?

_____

All-Star 4 Study Guide for Post-Testing Copyright © McGraw-Hill

All-Star 4 Study Guide

Student Name _____   Date _____

Instructor Name _____

See Workbook page 53.

Identify OSHA safety procedures at work. Workbook page 52. LCP-E 70.05

A Test your knowledge of workers' health and safety by taking the quiz below. Check (✓) your guesses. Then compare answers by looking on Workbook page 165.

Workers' Health and Safety Quiz

1. Workers in the United States have certain basic health and safety rights. Which of the following is NOT one of your rights at work?

   ☐ to remove uncomfortable safety equipment

   ☐ to report safety problems to OSHA (Occupational Safety & Health Administration)

   ☐ to get payment for medical care if you get hurt on the job

   ☐ to get health and safety training

   ☐ to see the record of injuries at your workplace

2. The most common workplace injuries are _____.

   ☐ chemical burns   ☐ cuts, lacerations

   ☐ fractures   ☐ sprains, strains

3. True or False? Your boss can fire you for refusing to do unsafe work.

   ☐ true   ☐ false

4. Which industry has the most workplace fatalities?

   ☐ construction   ☐ automotive

   ☐ mining   ☐ farming

5. True or False? Office workers don't have to worry about getting injured at work.

   ☐ true   ☐ false

B Read questions 1 to 5. Then read the story on page 53 and look for answers to the questions. Write your answers in complete sentences on the lines below.

1. How did James Wright get hurt?

   _____

2. How serious were his injuries?

   _____

3. How old is he now?

   _____

4. What advice does Wright have for workers?

   _____

5. Why do you think Wright didn't ask his boss for safety training?

   _____

All-Star 4 Study Guide

Student Name _____   Date _____

Instructor Name _____

★ ★

TAKE IT OUTSIDE: Interview someone you know who has a job. Ask the questions below and record the person's answers. Then tell your classmates what you learned.

Questions	Answers
1) What kind of work do you do?	
2) What kinds of hazards are at your job?	
3) What kind of safety training did you get for your job?	
4) Do you wear any protective clothing?	
5) What are the most common types of injuries at your workplace?	

★ ★

TAKE IT ONLINE: Use your favorite search engine to look for OSHA's website. Then list 3 new things you learned about this organization from the website.

1. _____

2. _____

3. _____

All-Star 4 Study Guide

Student Name _____   Date _____

Instructor Name _____

A Number each conversation in order starting with #1. Then add the information from the conversations to the appointment calendar below.

Conversation A

_____ Yes, the fifth would work fine.

_____ Yes, I have.

_____ I'm calling to set up an appointment.

_____ Yes. It's 555-9904.

_____ Have you been here before?

_____ I'm sorry, that was the 15th, not the 5th.

_____ Your name please?

_____ Yes, that's right. Can I have your phone number, please?

_____ Could you come in at noon on the 15th, Ms. James?

_____ The 15th? Oh, that's fine too. You said noon?

___1___ Dr. Ray's Office. How can I help you?

_____ It's James. Beverly James.

Conversation B

_____ Okay. Let me look for a morning appointment. What about the 15th at 8:30?

_____ And when would you like to come in?

_____ Yes, this is Chris Ma calling. I need to change an appointment I have with Dr. Ray.

_____ And when is your appointment?

___1___ Dr. Ray's office.

_____ It's this coming Friday at nine.

_____ That would be perfect.

_____ Does she have any openings next week?

_____ No, that won't work. I can only come in the morning.

_____ Let me see. Yes, she has an opening on the 12th at 2. Would you like that?

_____ And your telephone number is 555-8847?

_____ Yes, that's correct.

Conversation C

_____ I think it was 11 o'clock.

_____ What day was your appointment?

_____ Yes, this in Juanita Perez calling. I need to cancel an appointment.

_____ And the time?

_____ It was on the 15th.

_____ Yes, I see it now. Do you want to reschedule that?

___1___ Dr. Ray's office. Can I help you?

_____ Not right now, thank you. I'll call back later.

Appointments Calendar			⊠ ⊟ ⊞

Date: May 15, 2006 ▼   **Doctor:** Ray, Sylvia ▼

Start Time	Patient's Name	Procedure	Home Phone
08:30			
09:00	Oscar Hernandez	Follow-up	555-8574
09:30	Paul Smith	VAC	555-4586
10:00			
10:30	Sara Chang	EXAM	555-4733
11:00	Juanita Perez	Regular Visit	555-9955
11:30			
12:00			
12:30			

Demonstrate ability to give and request information clearly by telephone. Workbook page 46. LCP-E 74.02 ... CASAS 2.1.8

All-Star 4 Study Guide

Student Name _____   Date _____

Instructor Name _____

See Student Book page 43.

Communicate effectively using vocabulary related to doctors, dentists, body parts, illnesses, and medications. *BEST Plus: Describe similarities and differences between going to the doctor in the U.S. versus country of origin.* Student Book page 42. LCP-E 75.01 ... CASAS 3.1.1, 3.1.2, 3.1.3 ... BEST Plus

THINGS TO DO

1 Warm Up

Work with your classmates to answer these questions.

1. Do you know anyone who works as a health care professional? What does this person do?

2. Circle one of the health professionals on page 42 or 43 that you or someone you know has visited. What happened?

2 Read and Take Notes

Read the information about the 12 health care professionals on pages 42–43 and make a chart like this with 12 rows. Complete the chart. Then answer the questions below.

Health care professional	Specialty
1. *Cardiologist*	*treats heart diseases*
2.	

1. Which of the health care professionals in the chart is a medical doctor?

2. What are the similarities and differences between a respiratory therapist and a physical therapist? A psychiatrist and a psychologist?

3 Apply

Read about the people below and answer the questions.

1. Jeb frequently feels **depressed** and last night he told a friend that he had thoughts about dying. What kind of doctor might be able to help Jeb?

2. Sharon just moved to a new area and she needs to find a doctor for her 5-year-old son. What kind of doctor should she look for?

3. Soon after hip surgery, Hamid's doctor wanted him to start walking again. Who could help Hamid walk?

4. Marta gets her teeth cleaned twice a year. Who does this for her?

BEST *Plus:* Is going to the doctor in the U.S. the same or different from going to the doctor in your country?

All-Star 4 Study Guide

Student Name _____   Date _____

Instructor Name _____

See Student Book pages 42–43.

All-Star 4 Study Guide for Post-Testing Copyright © McGraw-Hill

---

Reading: FAQs about Heart Attacks

A. Look at the Big Picture. Read the FAQs and write the number(s) of the appropriate picture after each one.

A. What should you do if you think you or someone else is having a heart attack?
Call 911 immediately. Don't delay seeking medical help. Quick treatment can reduce the damage caused by the heart attack.   _____

B. Should you go to the doctor's office or the emergency room?
You should call 911 and have emergency personnel come as quickly as possible. Emergency personnel are usually trained to give medications and other treatments that may save your life.   _____

C. What are the symptoms of a heart attack?
The symptoms of a heart attack can vary. Many people feel a tightness or heaviness in the chest or chest pain. Others feel tingling or numbness in their left arm. Women sometimes have different symptoms, often complaining of nausea and trouble breathing.   _____

D. Are heart attacks mostly a problem for men?
No, women have heart attacks too, but they don't always recognize the symptoms.   _____

E. How are heart attacks treated?
If you get to the hospital within a few hours of the heart attack, you can be treated with medicines that dissolve blood clots. Such medications can help you avoid surgery to repair the damage and can restore blood flow.   _____

F. How can I prevent a heart attack?
The best way to avoid future heart attacks is to eat foods low in fat, exercise, and avoid stress.   _____

B. Circle *True* or *False*.

1. Heart attacks don't really affect women.	True	False
2. Once you have the heart attack the damage is done.	True	False
3. You should call your doctor if you have a heart attack.	True	False
4. The primary symptom of a heart attack is chest pain.	True	False
5. You shouldn't call 911 unless you are sure it's a heart attack.	True	False

Communicate effectively using vocabulary related to doctors, dentists, body parts, illnesses, and medications. *BEST Plus: Describe similarities and differences between going to the doctor in the U.S. versus country of origin.* Teacher's Edition page 188. LCP-E 75.01 . . . CASAS 3.1.1, 3.1.2, 3.1.3 . . . BEST *Plus*

BEST *Plus:* Is going to the doctor in the U.S. the same or different from going to the doctor in your country?

Unit 3   **27**

All-Star 4 Study Guide

Student Name _____   Date _____

Instructor Name _____

Follow emergency procedures and complete medical forms and accident report. Workbook page 43. LCP-E 75.02 . . . CASAS 3.2.1

C Read the information and answer the questions below.

When Should You Go to the Emergency Room?

At 7 in the morning, Ted suddenly felt a squeezing pain in the center of his chest. The pain then spread to his shoulders, neck, and arms. Ted thought he was going to faint, so he called to his wife, Nancy. Nancy wanted to call for an ambulance, but Ted asked her to wait awhile. Thirty minutes later, Ted didn't feel any better, so he asked Nancy to drive him to the hospital. By the time they arrived at the hospital, Ted was having trouble breathing. By the time Nancy stopped the car at the entrance to the emergency room, Ted was having a major heart attack. Nancy says she wishes she had called 911 and gotten Ted to the hospital right away, but like most people Ted didn't want to go and Nancy wasn't sure it was an emergency situation.

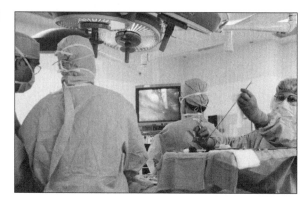

It's not always easy to know when to go to the emergency room, but if you are in doubt, it's always better to be safe than sorry. In most areas, you should dial 911 if you think someone needs emergency help. For some kinds of emergencies, every minute can make the difference between life and death, so don't delay.

If you take someone with a non-life-threatening problem to the emergency room, you can help make sure the patient is taken care of properly. The patient will need to check in with the triage nurse in the emergency room. The triage nurse will assess the patient's condition to determine how serious it is. The patient will also need to provide information about his or her medical history, drug allergies, medications, and health insurance coverage. While you are waiting in the emergency room, you should also watch for any changes in the patient's condition; let the nurse know if the person seems to be getting worse.

1. What were Ted's symptoms?

    _____

    _____

2. What should Nancy have done?

    _____

    _____

3. What does a triage nurse do?

    _____

    _____

4. What information do patients need to provide when they go to the emergency room?

    _____

    _____

All-Star 4 Study Guide

Student Name _____   Date _____

Instructor Name _____

See Student Book pages 46–47.

Read and interpret nutritional information listed on food labels and plan balanced diets. BEST Plus: State opinion about what people can do to stay healthy. State opinion about exercise. Student Book page 46. LCP-E 75.03 . . . CASAS 3.3.1, 3.3.2 . . . BEST Plus

THINGS TO DO

1 Warm Up

Work with your classmates to answer the questions below.

1. How often do you read the nutritional information on food labels?
2. Why do you think the U.S. government requires nutritional information on food labels?
3. Is your diet very healthy, somewhat healthy, or not very healthy? Why? Describe your diet.

2 Read and Compare

Study the food labels and read the sentences below. Then check (✓) *Peanuts* or *Spinach*.

	Label 1 Peanuts	Label 2 Spinach
1. Which food has more calories per serving?	☐	☐
2. Which has more calories from fat?	☐	☐
3. Which provides more calcium?	☐	☐
4. Which has more servings per **container**?	☐	☐
5. Which provides more Vitamin A?	☐	☐
6. Which has more sodium?	☐	☐
7. Which food has no cholesterol?	☐	☐
8. Which has more protein?	☐	☐

3 Apply

Work with a classmate to answer the questions below. Then compare answers with your classmates.

1. June ate two servings of peanuts. How many calories did she consume?
2. Climbing stairs for 10 minutes uses 100 calories. How many minutes do you have to climb stairs to burn a serving of peanuts?
3. Paul needs to **cut back on** the amount of fat in his diet. Do you think he should eat fewer vegetables? Why or why not?
4. Mei is worried that her children are not getting enough vitamins in their diet, so she gives them a handful of peanuts for their snack every day. Do you think this is a good idea? Why or why not?
5. Laura's cardiologist told her to eat foods with less fat. Based on that, should she eat less spinach or fewer peanuts?

Peanuts are high in protein.

All-Star 4 Study Guide

Student Name _____   Date _____

Instructor Name _____

Read and interpret nutritional information listed on food labels and plan balanced diets. *BEST Plus: State opinion about what people can do to stay healthy. State opinion about exercise.* Workbook page 49. LCP-E 75.03 . . . CASAS 3.3.1, 3.3.2 . . . BEST Plus

B Study the food labels and answer the questions below.

REDUCED FAT MILK
2% Milkfat

Nutrition Facts
Serving Size 1 cup (236ml)
Servings Per Container 1

Amount Per Serving

Calories 120   Calories from Fat 45

	% Daily Value*
Total Fat 5g	8%
Saturated Fat 3g	15%
Trans Fat 0g	
Cholesterol 20mg	7%
Sodium 120mg	5%
Total Carbohydrate 11g	4%
Dietary Fiber 0g	0%
Sugars 11g	
Protein 9g	17%

Vitamin A 10%   •   Vitamin C 4%
Calcium 30% • Iron 0% • Vitamin D 25%

*Percent Daily Values are based on a 2,000 calorie diet. Your daily values may be higher or lower depending on your calorie needs.

CHOCOLATE NONFAT MILK

Nutrition Facts
Serving Size 1 cup (236ml)
Servings Per Container 1

Amount Per Serving

Calories 80   Calories from Fat 0

	% Daily Value*
Total Fat 0g	0%
Saturated Fat 0g	0%
Trans Fat 0g	
Cholesterol Less than 5mg	0%
Sodium 120mg	5%
Total Carbohydrate 11g	4%
Dietary Fiber 0g	0%
Sugars 11g	
Protein 9g	17%

Vitamin A 10%   •   Vitamin C 4%
Calcium 30% • Iron 0% • Vitamin D 25%

*Percent Daily Values are based on a 2,000 calorie diet. Your daily values may be higher or lower depending on your calorie needs.

1. How many servings are there in a container of reduced fat milk? _____

2. Which type of milk has more calories per serving—reduced fat milk or chocolate nonfat milk?
   _____

3. Which has more fat per serving—reduced fat milk or chocolate nonfat milk? _____

4. Which has more cholesterol—reduced fat milk or chocolate nonfat milk? _____

5. How many glasses of nonfat milk would you need to drink daily to get the recommended amount of Vitamin D? _____

All-Star 4 Study Guide

Student Name _____   Date _____

Instructor Name _____

A Read questions 1 to 4. Then read the story below and look for answers to the questions. Write your answers on the lines.

1. What is an addiction?

   _____

2. Why did the writer think she was addicted to the computer?

   _____

3. What problems do you think the writer's addiction caused for her?

   _____

4. What are three more things you could do to stop this type of addiction?

   _____ *sell your computer* _____   _____

   _____   _____

Was I Addicted to the Computer?

by Tina Chang

I think I was addicted to the computer when I was in my second year of high school. At that time, the first thing that I did after school was turn on the computer. I would spend a lot of time checking my email even though I didn't get very many email messages. I spent hours and hours in front of my computer screen and surfed the Internet for a long time. Though I knew I should stop to do my homework, I just couldn't.

This situation lasted[1] for about two months, and then I became aware that I was spending too much time online. It was not easy to break the habit, but I still tried hard to do so. Now I am no longer addicted to the computer; I spend less than one hour in front of the computer screen each day.

Source: "Was I Addicted to the Computer?" by Tina Chang, *TOPICS* Online Magazine, www.topics-mag.com. Used by permission of TOPICS Online Magazine.

---
[1] lasted: continued

Recognize problems related to substance/drug abuse, and identify where treatment may be obtained. *BEST Plus: State opinion about illicit drug use among American teens and how to educate people about drugs.* Workbook page 54. LCP-E 75.04 . . . CASAS 2.5.3, 3.3.1, 3.3.3, 3.4.5 . . . BEST *Plus*

BEST *Plus:* How can we educate the public and children about health issues? How can we educate children and teens about the dangers of drug use?

All-Star 4 Study Guide

Student Name _____   Date _____

Instructor Name _____

Recognize requirements for immunizations. Student Book pages 50–51. LCP-E 75.05 . . . CASAS 3.2.2

1 Warm Up

Work with your classmates to answer the questions below.

1. When was the last time you got a shot? What was it for?
2. When you got your last shot, did it hurt?
3. Read the dictionary definition below. What is the noun form of the word *vaccinate*?

> **vaccinate** *v.* **-nated, -nating, -nates** to give someone a shot with medicine to prevent them from getting a disease: *The nurse vaccinated all of the children against the measles. -n.* **vaccination**

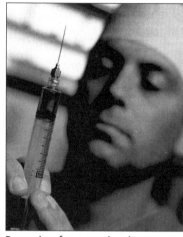

Preparing for a vaccination

2 Read and Respond

Read this information and answer the questions.

FAQs about Immunizations

1. Why should children be immunized?
Children need **immunizations** (shots) to protect them from dangerous childhood diseases such as **measles** and **mumps**. Most newborn babies are immune to many diseases because of antibodies they get from their mother. However, this immunity lasts for only about a year.

2. Why do adults sometimes need to be immunized?
- Some adults were never vaccinated as children.
- Newer vaccines were not available when some adults were children.
- Immunity can begin to fade over time. For example, it is **recommended** that adults get a tetanus and diphtheria shot every 10 years.
- As we age, we become more **susceptible** to serious disease caused by common infections (e.g., flu, pneumococcus).

3. What are the possible side effects of immunizations?
It is extremely unusual to have a **serious reaction** to a vaccine. Depending on the type of vaccine, however, a person might develop a slight fever, a soreness at the site of the shot, or a rash.

4. Is it possible to get free vaccinations?
Children without health insurance coverage can get free vaccines through a government program.

5. Does my child have to be immunized?
Not all states require immunization, but some states and local school districts do. Currently, some states allow refusal of immunization due to religious or personal reasons. Deciding to immunize or not is a serious decision.

Source: Centers for Disease Control and Prevention

> **FAQs = Frequently Asked Questions**

QUESTIONS

1. Why don't newborn babies need immunizations?
2. What is one example of a dangerous disease that children can get?
3. How long will a vaccination protect you from disease?
4. How likely is it for someone to have a serious reaction to a vaccination?
5. What are some possible side effects of a vaccination?

All-Star 4 Study Guide for Post-Testing Copyright © McGraw-Hill

All-Star 4 Study Guide

Student Name _____   Date _____

Instructor Name _____

A Eight punctuation marks are missing from the article below. Write the correct punctuation mark in each circle.

Taking Care of Your Health

People in the U.S. pay for their own medical care. Medical care is expensive ◯ so many people buy health insurance. You should get health insurance for yourself and your family as soon as possible.

Employers may offer health insurance as a benefit to their employees. Some employers pay all of your monthly health insurance fee ◯ and some pay only part of the fee. This monthly fee is called a "premium." You may need to pay part of the premium ◯ Usually ◯ employers will deduct the employee's part of the premium from their paycheck.

Doctors send their bills to your health insurance company. The health insurance company will pay for some or all of your medical bills. This is sometimes called a "co-payment. ◯

If you do not have health insurance ◯ you may be able to get federal or state health care assistance. In general ◯ most states provide some type of assistance to children and pregnant women. Check with the public health department of your state or town.

If you need urgent medical care ◯ you can go to the emergency room of the nearest hospital. Most hospitals are required by federal law to treat patients with a medical emergency even if the person cannot pay.

Source: http://uscis.gov/

B Read the article in Activity A and answer the questions below.

1. Why is it important to buy health insurance in the United States?

   _____

   _____

2. What is a "co-payment"?

   _____

   _____

3. If you don't have medical insurance, what should you do if you have a medical emergency?

   _____

   _____

Compare/contrast various types of insurance policies (life, health, homeowner's, renter's, vehicle). Workbook page 60. LCP-E 79.04 . . . CASAS 1.4.6, 1.9.8, 3.2.3

All-Star 4 Study Guide

Student Name _____ **Date** _____

Instructor Name _____

Utilize new vocabulary by context. Student Book page 55. LCP-E 83.06

2 Use context clues to guess the general meaning of the underlined words. Write your ideas on the lines. Then compare ideas with your classmates.

1. <u>Side effects</u> can occur with any medicine, including vaccines. Depending on the vaccine, these can include: slight fever, rash, or soreness at the site of the injection.

    unwanted effects from a medicine _____

2. If your child has a <u>severe</u> reaction to a vaccine, call your doctor right away.

    _____

3. The %DV shows you how much of the recommended daily amount of a <u>nutrient</u> (fat, sodium, fiber, etc.) is in a serving of that food.

    _____

4. Many things in your home can be poisonous if they are <u>swallowed</u>. These can include cleaning products, medicine, paint, alcohol, and cosmetics.

    _____

5. In the U.S., there are federal, state, and local law enforcement agencies that protect the public. In your community, law enforcement officers are the police or <u>sheriff</u>.

    _____

6. If you need a blood <u>transfusion</u> during surgery, you can use your own blood if you get it saved at least a week before surgery.

    _____

7. A <u>profusion</u> of recent research shows that aspirin may be good for more than headaches. The numerous new findings suggest that aspirin may also help prevent heart attacks and certain types of cancer.

    _____

8. In its regular form, aspirin is an <u>analgesic</u>—a painkilling drug—available without a prescription.

    _____

9. Many pills come in <u>buffered</u> form. The coating makes pills easier to swallow and easier on the stomach than tablets.

    _____

10. The American Lung Association reports a dramatic rise in the number of Americans with <u>asthma</u>. As many as 12 million Americans currently suffer from this lung condition, which blocks airflow and makes breathing difficult.

    _____

11. If both parents suffer from an allergy, their child has a 50 to 75 percent chance of <u>inheriting</u> it.

    _____

All-Star 4 Study Guide for Post-Testing Copyright © McGraw-Hill

All-Star 4 Study Guide

Student Name _____   Date _____

Instructor Name _____

Interpret statistical information from diagrams, tables, graphs, charts, and schedules. Workbook page 55. LCP-E 83.13 . . . CASAS 6.6.5

B Use the graph below to complete these sentences.

1. Alcohol is involved in _____ of the fatalities on highways.

2. More than _____ of the deaths in fires are alcohol related.

3. _____ of the accidents at work are alcohol related.

4. Alcohol was involved in _____ of the deaths of pedestrians.

How Alcohol Harms Society

Drinking too much not only harms individuals but society as a whole. Here is how alcohol abuse is related to many of our nation's most difficult problems. The numbers represent the percentage of all cases that are related to alcohol.

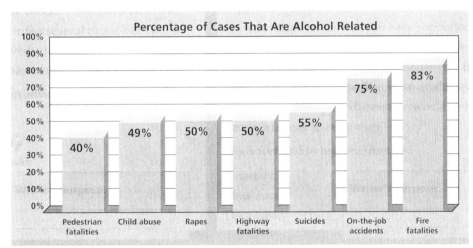

Source: "Percentage of Cases That Are Alcohol-Related", from Prevention's *Giant Book of Health Facts*, Rodale Press, 1991.

C What kinds of problems can each of these addictions cause for individuals, families, and communities? List 3 ideas for each category.

Drinking Alcohol	Gambling	Smoking	Taking Illegal Drugs
car accidents accidents at work bad health			

TAKE IT ONLINE: Use your favorite search engine to find the information below. Write down the addresses of the sites and share them with your classmates.

1. Find a site that gives information about treatments for addictions.

2. Find a site that gives information about drug abuse signs and symptoms.

3. Find a site that gives information about alcohol addiction.

All-Star 4 Study Guide

Student Name _____   Date _____

Instructor Name _____

Write a paragraph focusing on one topic (narration, definition, description, cause and effect). Workbook page 61. LCP-E 83.15

C Add the missing punctuation to the personal letters below.

September 12 2005

Dear Tricia

My apologies for not
returning your book sooner I
enjoyed it a lot and I thank
you for recommending it to me

Sincerely

Chandra

October 15 2006

Dear Phil and Ben

Please forgive me for not
writing sooner to thank you for
the beautiful flowers you sent
when I was in the hospital It
was very thoughtful of you to
think of me and having the
flowers cheered me up

My best
Oscar

D Write a letter to someone you know. Remember to punctuate your letter correctly.

All-Star 4 Study Guide

Student Name _____   Date _____

Instructor Name _____

Write complex and compound sentences with correct terminology and punctuation. Student Book page 56. LCP-E 83.16

IDENTIFYING PUNCTUATION MARKS

Punctuation marks are like road signs. They help your reader follow your ideas. Here are the names of some important punctuation marks.

In Written Materials

apostrophe	'	comma	,	hyphen	-
quotation marks	" "	period	.	bullet point	•
question mark	?	parentheses	( )	colon	:
exclamation point	!	slash	/	semicolon	;

On a Computer (when talking about a website or an email address)

back slash	\	dash	–	"at" mark	@
forward slash	/	underscore	_	dot	.

On a Phone (on an automated telephone message)

pound	#	star	*

1 Count and identify the punctuation marks in each sentence below.

1. A first aid kit has items you can use for small injuries or for pain, such as bandages, antiseptic wipes, instant ice packs, and gloves. _4 commas and 1 period_

2. If you need help during the night, call Dr. Fanning-White at (800) 555-2255.
   _____

3. You can get more information at http://www.redcross.org. This is called a "url."
   _____

4. The recording said, "Using the number keys on your phone, enter your credit card number followed by the # key." _____

5. Do <u>not</u> call 911 to do the following:
   • Ask for directions.
   • Ask for information about public services. _____

2 Write the correct punctuation marks in the sentences below.

1. The doctor▮s patient didn▮t arrive on time▮

2. Can you email me at drfranklin▮help▮net▮

3. My next appointment is on 03▮21▮07. That▮s the first day of spring▮

4. You can find information about immunizations at http▮▮▮www▮cde▮gov▮

5. When she saw the child run into the street, she yelled, "Stop▮"

All-Star 4 Study Guide

Student Name _____   Date _____

Instructor Name _____

Complete as much of the sample W-2 form as possible with information from the pay stub.

Sample W-2 Form: Wage and Tax Statement

a Control number	22222		OMB No. 1545-0008		
b Employer identification number			1 Wages, tips, other compensation		2 Federal income tax withheld
c Employer's name, address, and ZIP code			3 Social security wages		4 Social security tax withheld
			5 Medicare wages and tips		6 Medicare tax withheld
			7 Social security tips		8 Allocated tips
d Employee's social security number			9 Advance EIC payment		10 Dependent care benefits
e Employee's first name and initial Last name			11 Nonqualified plans		12a
			13 Statutory employee Retirement plan Third-party sick pay		12b
			14 Other		12c
					12d
f Employee's address and ZIP code					
15 State Employer's state ID number	16 State wages, tips, etc.		17 State income tax	18 Local wages, tips, etc.	19 Local income tax	20 Locality name

Form **W-2** Wage and Tax Statement   **2004**   Department of the Treasury—Internal Revenue Service
Copy 1—For State, City, or Local Tax Department

Sample Pay Stub

FASHION SOLUTIONS, INC.

Employee: Julia Smith
Social Security Number: 123-45-6789   Check Number: **56499543**
Pay Period Date: 10/01/05 to 10/15/05
Check Date: 10/20/05

EARNINGS	Rate	Hours	This Period	Year-to-Date
	15.00	80	1,200.00	22,800.00
GROSS PAY			1,200.00	22,800.00
DEDUCTIONS				
Federal Income Tax			156.00	2,964.00
Social Security			132.00	2,508.00
Medicare			31.20	592.80
CA Income Tax			36.13	684.47
CA State Disability Ins.			16.80	319.20
Total Deductions			372.13	7,069.27
NET PAY			827.87	

All-Star 4 Study Guide

Student Name _____ Date _____

Instructor Name _____

---

1 Warm Up

Look over the information in Activity 2 and answer the questions below.

1. Where is the information from—a newspaper, a book, a website, or a magazine? How do you know?
2. What kind of organization do you think the AFL-CIO is?

2 Read and Respond

Read the information below and answer the questions.

☒ ⊟ ⊞ **AFL-CIO**

[SEARCH _____] [GO]   Site Quick Find: [▾]   **AFL-CIO**

| **All About Unions** | **Issues & Politics** | **Jobs, Wages & the Economy** | **About the AFL-CIO** | **Media Center** |

Home >> All About Unions >> How & Why People Join Unions

- Labor Day
- *Voice@Work*
- Form Your Union
- How & Why People Join Unions
  - Unions 101
  - What Unions Do
  - Myths and Facts about Unions
- Workers' Voices
- Local Union Movements
- Global Unions

How & Why People Join Unions

1 People who **work for a living** know about the inequality of power between employers and employees. Workers want to form unions so they can have a voice on the job to improve their lives, their families, and their communities.

2 With a union, working people win basic rights, like a **say** in their jobs, safety and **security**. Unions help **remedy** discrimination because union contracts ensure that all workers are treated fairly and equally. When there's a problem on the job, workers and management can work together as equals to solve it.

3 Unions help make sure our nation prioritizes working people's issues: unions hold corporations **accountable**, make workplaces safe, protect Social Security and retirement, fight for quality health care and ensure that working people have time to spend with their families. All workers **deserve** to make a free and fair decision on whether to form a union.

Why People Join Unions

4 A union is a group of workers who come together to win respect on the job, better wages and benefits, more flexibility for work and family needs and a voice in improving the quality of their products and services.

Source: http://www.aflcio.org/aboutunions/joinunions/

QUESTIONS

1. What is a union?

_____

2. What is the purpose of a union?

_____

3. What basic rights can a union help workers win?

_____

4. In paragraph 4, which issue is the most important to you?

_____

Demonstrate understanding of worker's rights (compensation, unionization, right to work). Student Book pages 68–69. LCP-E 70.04 . . . CASAS 4.2.2

All-Star 4 Study Guide

Student Name _____   Date _____

Instructor Name _____

See Workbook page 73.

Identify and explain common problems and solutions. Workbook page 72. LCP-E 73.02 . . . . CASAS 7.3.1, 7.3.2, 7.3.3

A Whose responsibility is it? Check (✓) *Landlord* or *Tenant*.

Whose responsibility is it to _____?	the landlord	the tenant
1. provide locks and keys for doors	☐	☐
2. get rid of insects, rodents, etc.	☐	☐
3. put trash in trash cans	☐	☐
4. repair the heating system if it breaks	☐	☐
5. provide smoke detectors	☐	☐
6. keep the rental property clean so it doesn't attract insects, rodents, etc.	☐	☐
7. replace batteries in smoke detectors	☐	☐

B Read each person's problem below. Then use the information on page 73 to answer each person's question.

1. I live in a large apartment building and I often see the landlord go into people's apartments when they are not at home. My neighbor even came home one day when the landlord was in the apartment. He told her he was checking the smoke detectors. Does he really have the right to enter our apartments whenever he wants to? What can we do? —Stella Problem: Possible response:	2. The shower in my apartment doesn't work properly. I told my landlord about it three weeks ago, but he still hasn't fixed it. I have left him several messages on his answering machine but he hasn't returned my calls. What should I do? —Hamid Problem: Possible response:
3. During the summer my landlord sometimes turns the electricity off. He says he is only doing this to make repairs but I know this isn't true. What can I do? —Z.B. Problem: Possible response:	4. There's something wrong with the refrigerator in our apartment. We told the landlord about it and he promised to either fix it or buy us a new one. That was two months ago and still nothing has happened. What can we do? —Taka Problem: Possible response:

All-Star 4 Study Guide

Student Name _____   Date _____

Instructor Name _____

B Read this information and answer the questions below.

The Bill of Rights

The first ten amendments, or changes, to the U.S. Constitution protect certain freedoms and rights of U.S. citizens by limiting the power of the government. These ten amendments are called The Bill of Rights.

First Amendment Guarantees the rights of freedom of speech, religion, press, peaceable assembly, and to petition the government.

Second Amendment Guarantees the right to bear arms.

Third Amendment Says the government cannot force citizens to house soldiers in their homes during peacetime and without permission.

Fourth Amendment States that the government cannot search or take a person's property without a warrant.

Fifth Amendment Says that a person cannot be tried twice for the same crime or forced to testify against himself or herself.

Sixth Amendment States that people have the right to a fair trial with adequate legal representation.

Seventh Amendment Guarantees a trial by jury in most cases.

Eighth Amendment Prohibits all "cruel and unusual punishment."

Ninth Amendment Says that people have other rights in addition to those listed in the Constitution.

Tenth Amendment States that the powers that the Constitution does not give to the national government belong to the states and to the citizens.

1. Which amendment says you have other rights, in addition to those listed in the Constitution? _____

2. Which amendment allows you to disagree with an action of the government? _____

3. Which amendment prevents the government from telling newspapers what to print? _____

4. Which amendment prevents the government from forcing people to go church? _____

5. Which amendment says the government cannot enter your house without a strong reason? _____

6. Which amendment prevents the government from stopping a protest march? _____

Demonstrate understanding of selected U.S. historical traditions and common social customs. Workbook page 65. LCP-E 80.01 . . . CASAS 2.7.1, 2.7.2, 2.7.3 . . . BEST *Plus*

All-Star 4 Study Guide

Student Name _____   Date _____

Instructor Name _____

Interact with community services, organizations, and government agencies.
Workbook page 69. LCP-E 80.02 . . . CASAS 2.5.2, 2.5.3, 2.5.5, 2.5.6, 2.5.9 . . . BEST *Plus*

C Read the information from a website. Use it to answer the questions below.

⊠⊟⊞   **www.osha.gov**

U.S. Department of Labor
Occupational Safety & Health Administration
www.osha.gov

Search [_____] GO

Site Index: A B C D E F G H I J K L M N O P Q R S T U V W X Y Z

Making a Positive Difference

OSHA Saves Lives

1 "Get out of that trench," OSHA Inspector Robert Dickinson ordered a worker in an unsafe trench by the side of the road near El Paso, Texas. El Paso Assistant Area Director Mario Solano had noticed the trench earlier, and he sent Dickinson and Elia Casillas to check it out. Thirty seconds after the employee got out of the trench, the wall near where he had been standing collapsed. Warning the worker to leave the trench prevented the worker from experiencing a serious injury.

2 On June 10, OSHA compliance officers from the El Paso District Office helped prevent a terrible accident. The two officers were sent to the site of a tower under construction. At the construction site, the two officers found that workers on the tower did not have proper equipment to protect them from an 80 foot fall. The OSHA officers talked with the employer who then instructed the workers to get off the tower. The employer agreed to install a safety system to protect the workers from a fall.

3 In August, two workers were washing windows from a scaffold high up above the ground. Suddenly the scaffold broke, and the two men remained hanging in the air. Luckily the two workers were using the proper safety equipment and they didn't fall to the ground. Soon, the fire department was able to rescue them.

Source: http://www.osha.gov/

1. The information above is from the website of which government agency?

   _____

2. In the first story, why did the inspector tell the employee to get out of the trench?

   _____

3. In the second story, what was the problem with the tower?

   _____

4. In the second story, what did the employer need to do?

   _____

5. In the third story, why didn't the workers get hurt?

   _____

6. What do these three stories have in common?

   _____

7. How is the third story different from the first two?

   _____

All-Star 4 Study Guide for Post-Testing Copyright © McGraw-Hill

All-Star 4 Study Guide

Student Name _____   Date _____

Instructor Name _____

See Student Book page 74. Identify the writer's purpose for writing each letter.

2

4536 Santini Street
Jersey City, NJ 07306
April 12, 2006

Representative Robert Menendez
United States House of Representatives
2238 Rayburn House Office Building
Washington, D.C. 20515

Dear Representative Menendez:

I am writing to ask for help in getting my social security checks. I have written to the proper authorities several times, but I have not yet received a response. Please find enclosed copies of this correspondence.

I thank you in advance for your help.

Sincerely,

Sonya Bluvosky

Sonya Bluvosky

Writer's purpose:

_____

_____

3

642 South Beverly Dr.
Palm Springs, CA 92264
August 21, 2006

Congresswoman Mary Bono
404 Canon House Office Building
Washington D.C. 20515

Dear Congresswoman Bono:

I am writing to invite you to speak at a meeting of the Durham Voter's Network. The Voter's Network is a nonpartisan group that is interested in many of the environmental issues that you have supported in the past. Our members would especially be interested in hearing about the environmental issues you are currently working on in the House. If you are available on any of the dates on the attached sheet, we would be honored to have you speak to our group.

I look forward to hearing from you.

Sincerely,

Dora Lasky

Dora Lasky

Writer's purpose:

_____

_____

2 Identify an issue or problem in your community. For example: Do people drive too fast on streets with children? Is there too much graffiti or litter in public places? Do people play loud music late at night? Write a letter to the mayor of your town or city. Explain the problem and suggest a solution. Write your purpose in the box.

_____

_____

_____

_____

_____

_____

Writer's purpose:

_____

_____

Demonstrate ability to interact with local, state, and national officials and their functions.
Student Book page 75. LCP-E 80.03 . . .CASAS 5.5.8

All-Star 4 Study Guide

Student Name _____   Date _____

Instructor Name _____

See Student Book page 63.

Demonstrate knowledge of U.S. educational system (compulsory schooling, child care, PTA). *BEST Plus: State opinion about how children learn and what is important to learn at school.* Student Book page 62. LCP-E 82.01 . . . CASAS 2.5.5, 2.5.9 . . . *BEST Plus*

THINGS TO DO

1 Warm Up

Work with your classmates to answer the questions below.

1. What do you see people in the pictures doing?
2. Read the information in each box and answer the questions.
3. Study the bar graph on page 63. What is the relationship between level of education and income in the U.S.?

2 Listen and Take Notes 🎧

Listen to 6 people's opinions about education. Summarize each opinion.

Speaker's opinion	Agree	Disagree
1. *Parents should be involved in their child's school and education.*		
2.		
3.		
4.		
5.		
6.		

Check (✓) if you agree or disagree with each opinion.

3 Listen and Circle Your Answer 🎧

Listen to 5 conversations. Check (✓) if the people agree or disagree.

	#1	#2	#3	#4	#5
They agree.					
They disagree.					

BEST *Plus*: Where do the children in your area go to school? What do you think are the most important things children learn at school? Should parents be actively involved in their children's education? What is your opinion on that topic?

All-Star 4 Study Guide

Student Name _____   Date _____

Instructor Name _____

A Read these opinions and tell if you agree or disagree. Check (✓) your ideas.

1. In my opinion, all citizens should be required to vote in the presidential election.

   ☐ I think so too.   ☐ I'm not sure about that.

2. I wish they would raise the speed limit on highways.

   ☐ So do I.   ☐ You do?

3. I think health care should be free.

   ☐ Me too.   ☐ Really? Why is that?

4. I don't like to pay taxes.

   ☐ Neither do I.   ☐ Really? Why not?

5. I don't think children should have to go to school until they are 16.

   ☐ I don't either.   ☐ Really? Why is that?

6. I enjoy reading about history.

   ☐ I do too.   ☐ You do?

B Complete the conversations so that the people agree.

1. A: I think we should vote in the election tomorrow.

   B: _____

2. A: I don't think people should keep guns at home.

   B: _____

3. A: I think it's important to get a college education.

   B: _____

4. A: I think the voting age should be changed.

   B: _____

5. A: I don't think schools should sell junk food to children.

   B: _____

6. A: I think it's important to study history.

   B: _____

7. A: I prefer coeducational schools.

   B: _____

8. A: I think our public transportation system should be a lot better.

   B: _____

Demonstrate knowledge of U.S. educational system (compulsory schooling, child care, PTA). *BEST Plus: State opinion about how children learn and what is important to learn at school.* Workbook page 66. LCP-E 82.01 . . . CASAS 2.5.5, 2.5.9 . . . BEST *Plus*

BEST *Plus:* Where do the children in your area go to school? What do you think are the most important things children learn at school? Should parents be actively involved in their children's education? What is your opinion on that topic?

All-Star 4 Study Guide

Student Name _____   Date _____

Instructor Name _____

A Complete the questions with words from the box. Then answer the questions.

disasters	investigates	consumer
recall	obey	discrimination
acronym	enforces	

1. What does the _____ FEMA stand for?

   _____

2. Why might an automobile company _____ one of its cars?

   _____

3. Which U.S. government agency works to stop _____ at work?

   _____

4. What kinds of _____ does the Federal Emergency Management Agency help communities recover from?

   _____

5. What is the acronym for the _____ Product Safety Commission?

   _____

6. Which U.S. government agency _____ clean air laws?

   _____

7. Which U.S. agency _____ federal crimes?

   _____

8. Who makes sure that businesses _____ the law?

   _____

All-Star 4 Study Guide

Student Name _____   Date _____

Instructor Name _____

Use the information in the graph to answer the questions.

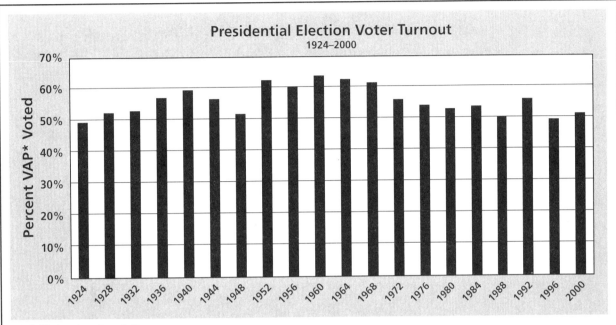

Presidential Election Voter Turnout
1924–2000

*VAP: Voting Age Population

6. In which year was voter turnout the highest?

A. 1932
B. 1940
C. 1960
D. 1980

7. In which year below was voter turnout the lowest?

A. 1928
B. 1948
C. 1996
D. 2000

8. Which statement is true?

A. In 1956, 60% of the people didn't vote.
B. The number of people who have voted has decreased steadily.
C. More people voted in 1940 than in 1924.
D. More people vote now than in the past.

9. What information is provided in the graph?

A. The percent of women who voted.
B. The percent of people who didn't vote.
C. The percent of people who voted.
D. The number of people who voted in each election.

10. In which two years was the voter turnout about the same?

A. 1948 and 2000
B. 1924 and 1960
C. 1988 and 1992
D. 1928 and 1964

All-Star 4 Study Guide

Student Name _____   **Date** _____

Instructor Name _____

See Student Book page 73. Read the information and complete Activity 1 and Activity 2.

ADJUSTING YOUR READING SPEED

Good readers are flexible. They change the way they read to match their reading goals.

Ways to Read

Skim. When you skim a text, you move your eyes quickly across the words. Skimming helps you to learn the topic of the text.

Scan. When you scan a text, you move your eyes quickly across the text to look for specific words or information. For example, you might scan the text for the names of countries or dates.

Read quickly. When you read quickly, you try to read groups of words together. You don't read each word separately.

Read slowly. When you come to a part of a text that you want to remember, you can read the information slowly and try to restate it in your own words.

5 Common Reading Goals

- to get the gist or general meaning
- to decide if you want to read something
- to find specific information
- to read for fun
- to learn and remember what you read

1 How would you read the following items? Check (✓) your answer. Answers will vary, depending on your reading goals.

	Skim	Scan	Read quickly	Read slowly
1. a chart with tonight's TV programs	✓	☐	☐	☐
2. a letter from your boss	☐	☐	☐	☐
3. a paycheck	☐	☐	☐	☐
4. instructions for taking a test	☐	☐	☐	☐
5. a funny story	☐	☐	☐	☐
6 a movie review	☐	☐	☐	☐
7. a very big bill	☐	☐	☐	☐
8. a newspaper article about you	☐	☐	☐	☐

Work with your classmates. Compare ideas and give reasons for your answers.

2 Follow the steps below to read the article on page 73.

Step 1. How interesting does the article look to you? Skim it and circle your answer.

Very interesting   Somewhat interesting   Not very interesting

Step 2. What is the topic of the article? Skim it again and write your answer below.

Topic: _____

Step 3: What numbers appear in the article? Scan the reading to find them.

Step 4: What is the writer's main idea? Read the article quickly and write your idea below.

Main Idea: _____

Step 5: Which paragraph in the article was the most interesting to you? _____ Read this part again slowly and then summarize it in your own words.

All-Star 4 Study Guide

Student Name _____   Date _____

Instructor Name _____

A Complete the questions below with the correct form of the word in the box. Then answer the questions.

NOUN	VERB	ADJECTIVE
1. authority	authorize	XXXXX
2. treatment	treat	XXXXX
3. honesty	XXXXX	honest
4. gathering	gather	XXXXX
5. religion	XXXXX	religious
6. belief	believe	believable
7. tolerance	tolerate	tolerant
8. registration	register	XXXXX
9. election	elect	XXXXX
10. respect	respect	respectful

1. In the United States, who has the _____ to make new laws?

   _____

2. What is an example of unfair _____ of an employee by an employer?

   _____

3. How can you tell when someone isn't being _____?

   _____

4. Where in your city do large groups of people sometimes _____?

   _____

5. What is the closest _____ building to your school?

   _____

6. Do you _____ everything you read in the newspaper?

   _____

7. What kind of behavior is difficult to _____?

   _____

8. Can you _____ to vote by mail?

   _____

Identify parts of speech and use in sentences. Workbook page 64. LCP-E 84.02

All-Star 4 Study Guide

Student Name _____   Date _____

Instructor Name _____

Active and Passive Verb Forms

A verb can be active or passive. In a sentence with an active verb, the subject does the action of the verb. In a sentence with a passive verb, the subject receives the action of the verb.

Subject	Active verb		Subject	Passive verb

The citizens **elect** the president.   The president **is elected** by the citizens.

It is common to use a passive verb when you don't know who did something.

> EXAMPLES: The school **is locked up** at night.
> All citizens **are encouraged** to vote.

You can use a passive verb to emphasize the action instead of the person who did the action. In these cases the passive verb is followed with *by* + a noun.

> EXAMPLES: New laws are passed **by Congress**.
> Children are required **by law** to attend school.

---

1 Identify

Read the sentences and write *A* (Active) or *P* (Passive).

1. __*A*__ The Bill of Rights spells out many of the rights of U.S. citizens.
2. _____ In the United States, citizens are not required to vote.
3. _____ Discrimination because of someone's race or age is illegal.
4. _____ U.S. citizens are allowed to follow any or no religion.
5. _____ Most public schools in the U.S. are coeducational, meaning that girls and boys study together.
6. _____ Employers are not allowed to pay their employees less than the minimum wage.
7. _____ In most states, parents are allowed to teach their children at home. This is called *home schooling*.
8. _____ What children learn at school is decided by the state.
9. _____ Education is paid for by income taxes and property taxes.
10. _____ The EPA enforces environmental laws.
11. _____ The FBI collects statistics on crime.

2 Choose the Correct Verb

Read the sentences and choose the active or passive verb form in parentheses. Write the verb in the blank.

1. Children _____ extracurricular activities after school. (do / is done)
2. Employees _____ a certain number of breaks during the work day. (give / are given)
3. In most states, children ages 5 to 16 _____ to go to school. (require / are required)
4. If your employer _____ you unfairly, you must report it. (treats / is treated)
5. After a disaster, communities _____ help from FEMA. (receive / is received)

All-Star 4 Study Guide

Student Name _____   Date _____

Instructor Name _____

B Complete these sentences.

1. If a store accepts only cash or credit card, you cannot pay by _____

2. If something is nonreturnable, you can't _____

3. If you lose the receipt for something you purchased, you can't _____

4. If a salesperson tries to pressure you into buying something, you can _____

5. If something comes with a warranty, you can _____

6. If you buy things in bulk, you can _____

7. If something is advertised "on sale" but is out of stock, you can _____

8. If you can't find something in a store, you should _____

C Read the information and complete the sentences below.

How are you going to pay for it?

When you decide to buy something, there are a number of different ways you can pay for it. You can always pay by cash, but that means you have to carry around a lot of money. Instead of cash, you can purchase some things by writing a personal check. To do this, however, you have to open a checking account at a bank. You also have to make sure you always have enough money in your account to cover your purchases.

Some stores will also give you a charge account. This allows you to "charge" or purchase things using your charge card. Every month the store sends you a bill for the things you bought. For some charge accounts you must pay the full amount at the end of the month. Some charge accounts, however, will allow you to make a minimum monthly payment. You only have to pay part of the bill at the end of the month, but you also have to pay interest on the amount of money you owe. Credit cards are another popular tool for buying things. Most credit cards allow you to make a minimum monthly payment, but they also charge a high interest rate.

Many stores also have layaway programs. If you don't have enough money to buy something, for example a new couch, you can put it on layaway. You make a down payment and the store holds the item for you. Then, usually over the next 30 to 90 days, you can pay the rest of the money.

1. One disadvantage of using cash to buy things is that _____

2. If you want to pay by personal check, you must _____

3. Credit card companies make money by _____

4. If you want to put something on layaway, you must first make _____

5. One advantage of using a layaway program to buy something is that _____

Demonstrate understanding of banking system (loans, interest rates, investments, mortgages), terms, foreign currencies, and exchange rates. *BEST Plus: Describe shopping preferences and state opinion about buying clothes. Describe preferences and methods of payment.* Workbook page 87. LCP-E 76.01 . . . CASAS 1.8.1, 1.8.2, 1.8.4 . . . *BEST Plus*

BEST *Plus:* How do you pay for your purchases (ATM, credit card, check, cash)?

All-Star 4 Study Guide

Student Name _____ Date _____

Instructor Name _____

Interpret classified ads and other resources to locate housing (lease or purchase). Student Book pages 86–87. LCP-E 79.01 . . . CASAS 1.4.2, 1.4.3

1 Warm Up

Work with your classmates to answer the questions below.

1. In addition to the newspaper, where can you find information about houses for rent?
2. What do you think is the best way to find a house or an apartment for rent?
3. What advice would you give to someone looking for a house for rent?

2 Read and Respond

Read this information and answer the questions.

Houses for Rent   453

North End, 2 BR, 2 baths on dead-end street. $1000/mo. + sec. dep. Call Karen 555-3590

2BR, newly remodeled, W/D hkup, 1.5 BA, no pets/smoking, $1200/mo. Patty or Sam 555-8998

2BR Ranch, Stv, frig, dshwshr, W/D include'd. Lg bkyard. $1200/mo. + utils. 555-5827

Exc. cond. 3 BR house, lrg deck & private setting $900/mo. Immed. occupancy. 555-3325

3 BR, 2.5 bath, 2 car gar, avail. 12/15, short term, no lease $1200/mo. Cell 555-0949

Contemporary 3 BR, 2 baths, cent. air, garage, pet ok. $1100/mo. Call Peter 555-3356

Nice 2 BR home w/porch & 2 stall garage, on lg. lot, $1100. No pets. Call Dick 555-2113

Condominium Rentals   457

2 BR, open concept, ample prkg. Inc. heat/hw/gas, central a/c. $900/mo. Call Jennifer 555-7867

Brand NEW condo. 6 rms, 2BR, central air. $1200/mo. Call Kathleen after 8 PM 555-3354

WEST SIDE Large 1 BR, new paint/carpet, pets ok, parking, a/c, ht & hw included $850/mo. 555-0878

Furnished Apartments   459

So. Beech. 1st flr, 1 BR/LR, kitchen, bath, prkg, deposit, $200/wk, incls all utils. 555-6584

2 1/2 rms, 1 bath, compl furn'd, no pets/smkrs, parkg & all utils provided. $750/mo. 555-4463

Unfurnished Apartments   461

WEST SIDE Lg 1 BR, include. Ht/HW, gar, porch. Nice yard, small dog ok. $800/mo. 555-9984

EAST SIDE. 2 BR completely renovated, off-st prkg, no utils., $900/mo. 555-6657

DOWNTOWN Lrg 2 BR, new windows, lndry., $675/mo. 555-9068

So. Beech. Safe nghbh'd, 1 BR, new windows/paint/flr. No smkg/pets. Landlord/credit refs checked. Avail. 2/1. $900/mo. 555-3256

EAST SIDE 2BR, nice area, nice bldg., storage room, owner occup'd bldg, no dogs, $800/mo. 555-3657

DOWNTOWN, super clean lg 2 BR, new kitchen, near hospital. 555-5884

Housing to Share   467

QUESTIONS

1. You are looking for a condo to rent. Which section of the want ads should you look at?
2. You want to rent an apartment that you will furnish. Which section would you look at?
3. You are looking for a house with 3 bedrooms to rent. Which number would you call?
4. You are looking for an apartment that allows pets. Which number would you call?
5. Choose 2 of the 1-bedroom apartments for rent. How are they similar and different?
6. Which ad looks the most interesting to you? Why?

All-Star 4 Study Guide for Post-Testing Copyright © McGraw-Hill

All-Star 4 Study Guide

Student Name _____   **Date** _____

Instructor Name _____

See Student Book page 86.

3 Apply.

Write a classified ad for your own house or apartment.

Interpret classified ads and other resources to locate housing (lease or purchase). Student Book page 87. LCP-E 79.01 . . . CASAS 1.4.2, 1.4.3

Unit 5

53

All-Star 4 Study Guide

Student Name _____   **Date** _____

Instructor Name _____

See Student Book page 83.

Compare/contrast advertisements, labels, and charts to select goods and services. *BEST Plus: Describe shopping preferences, payment, how TV and newspaper advertisements influence shopping decisions.*
Student Book page 82. LCP-E 79.03 . . . CASAS 1.2.1, 1.3.1, 1.3.5, 1.6.1 . . .BEST *Plus*

THINGS TO DO

1 Warm Up

Work with your classmates to answer these questions.

1. What's your favorite place to buy groceries? Why?
2. Which of these things do you use when you shop for groceries—coupons, store fliers, a grocery list?
3. Why is it a good idea to be a **comparison shopper**?

3 Compare

Use the store flyers to choose the store with the best price for each food below. Check (✓) your answers. Then compare ideas with your classmates.

Where is _____ cheaper?	Henry's	Foodbasket
pasta	☐	☐
grapes	☐	☐
toilet paper	☐	☐
_____	☐	☐

4 Write

Plan a meal for 20 people. Choose 4 items you need from the store flyers. Make a chart like this and answer the questions below.

Item	Quantity/Size	Henry's Price	Foodbasket Price
pasta	(12) 16 oz packages	$10.68	$8.00

1. How much would you spend if you bought all 4 items at Henry's?
2. How much would you spend if you bought all 4 items at the Foodbasket?
3. Which item on your list is the best bargain?

BEST *Plus:* Do you like to go shopping? Do you think advertisements on TV and in the newspaper influence what you buy?

All-Star 4 Study Guide

Student Name _____   Date _____

Instructor Name _____

2 Read and Respond

Read the food shopping tips and answer these questions.

1. In picture 1, which cereal is the better buy? Why?
2. In picture 2, which type of rice is the better deal?
3. Why do you think grocery stores put more expensive items at eye level?
4. What can you do if you find a mistake on a receipt?
5. What are 3 other grocery shopping tips?

FOOD SHOPPING TIPS

1 When you buy packaged food, be sure to check the **net weight**. A large box might have less in it than a small box.

2 Read the **unit price** when you are comparing different brands. The unit price, for example, the price per ounce, is usually listed on the store shelf. The store brands or the generic brands are often the cheapest.

3 More expensive items are often placed on the store shelf at eye level. Lower priced items of the same food are up higher or down lower.

4 Watch as the cashier **rings up** your purchase. The **scanners** at the checkout line don't always register the correct amount. Check your receipt and say something if you think there is a mistake.

BEST *Plus:* Do you like to go shopping? Do you think advertisements on TV and in the newspaper influence what you buy?

Compare/contrast advertisements, labels, and charts to select goods and services. BEST *Plus: Describe shopping preferences, payment, how TV and newspaper advertisements influence shopping decisions.*
Student Book pages 82–83. LCP-E 79.03 . . . CASAS 1.2.1, 1.3.1, 1.3.5, 1.6.1 . . . BEST *Plus*

All-Star 4 Study Guide

Student Name _____   Date _____

Instructor Name _____

Interact with community services, organizations, and government agencies.
Workbook page 94. LCP-E 80.02 . . . CASAS 2.5.2, 2.5.3, 2.5.5, 2.5.6, 2.5.9

A Use the list of Resources for Consumers below to answer these questions.

1. Which resource provides information about different types of insurance? _____

2. Which 3 resources are U.S. federal government agencies? _____ _____

   _____

3. Which federal agency would handle a complaint about false advertising? _____

4. What does the acronym HUD stand for? _____

5. How could you file a complaint with the FTC? _____

6. How can you get in touch with the ACLU? _____

Resources for Consumers

Consumers can get help from federal and state government agencies and from the many consumer advocacy groups. Here are just a few of the available resources:

The American Civil Liberties Union (ACLU)

The American Civil Liberties Union focuses on issues affecting individual freedom. To contact them, call a local ACLU office listed in your telephone directory.

Attorneys General

If you have a consumer issue involving the laws of your state, contact your state attorney general.

Better Business Bureaus (BBB)

The Council of Better Business Bureaus has more than 100 local offices nationwide. Check out a business or find out about the dispute resolution program. Look in your telephone book for the nearest BBB.

The Federal Communications Commission (FCC)

The Federal Communications Commission oversees interstate and international communications by radio, television, wire, satellite, and cable. To make a complaint or obtain information, call 888-CALL-FCC.

The Federal Trade Commission (FTC)

The Federal Trade Commission is responsible for enforcing numerous consumer protection laws focusing on deceptive and unfair trade practices.

To file a complaint or obtain information, call 877-FTC-HELP.

The U.S. Department of Housing and Urban Development (HUD)

The U.S. Department of Housing and Urban Development is responsible for handling complaints regarding housing discrimination, manufactured housing, and land sales.

INSURE.COM

This website provides consumer information and resources on life, health, car, and home insurance topics.

NOLO.COM

Nolo provides legal information for consumers on many different consumer topics; 800-728-3555.

Public Citizen

Founded by Ralph Nader, Public Citizen is a consumer advocacy organization that promotes consumer interest in energy, environment, trade, health, and government issues.

From "Resources for Consumers" from *Understanding Consumer Rights* by Nicolette Parsi and Marc Robinson, New York: Dorling Kindersley, 2000.

All-Star 4 Study Guide for Post-Testing Copyright © McGraw-Hill

All-Star 4 Study Guide

Student Name _____   Date _____

Instructor Name _____

See Workbook page 92.

B A customer and a store clerk are standing at the Information Desk of the store in Activity 1. Use the floor plan to complete the conversations below. Circle the best answer.

1. Customer: I'm looking for scissors.

   Clerk: Scissors? They are in with _____. (sewing supplies / sports equipment) That's behind the garden and yard supplies.

2. Customer: Do you sell brooms?

   Clerk: Yes, we do. They're in with _____ supplies. (pet / cleaning) That's aisle 7. Just go down that way past the _____ supplies. (automotive / plumbing)

3. Customer: Do you sell fishing rods?

   Clerk: Yes, we do. They are in aisle _____. (3 / 4) Just go down past the plumbing supplies on your left and you'll see the _____ on your right just after school supplies. (toys / sports equipment)

4. Customer: Do you carry those things to put paint on walls?

   Clerk: Do you mean a paint brush?

   Customer: Yes, a paint brush.

   Clerk: You'll find them just over there in aisle _____. (6 / 7)

5. Customer: Do you carry vacuum cleaner bags?

   Clerk: Yes, we do. They are at the end of aisle _____ in the cleaning supplies. (3 / 7)

   Customer: Thanks.

   Clerk: You're welcome.

6. Customer: Do you sell hoses?

   Clerk: Sure. They're in _____ supplies. They're at the end of the aisle near the entrance. (sewing / garden and yard)

   Customer: Thanks.

7. Customer: Can you tell me where the wrapping paper is?

   Clerk: Sure. It's in the gift section, next to the _____. (painting supplies / pet supplies)

8. Customer: Do you sell children's clothes?

   Clerk: _____. (Yes, we do. / No, I'm sorry, we don't.)

Listen and follow directions. Workbook page 93. LCP-E 83.01 . . . CASAS 2.5.4

Unit 5   **57**

All-Star 4 Study Guide

Student Name _____ **Date** _____

Instructor Name _____

Recognize sequence of events in a reading passage. Workbook page 86. LCP-E 83.07

A Number each conversation in order starting with number #1.

Conversation A

_____ Yes, we do—as long as you have another form of identification.

_____ Yes, I'd like to pay for these.

_____ Yes. That would be fine.

_____ Okay. How would you like to pay for them?

___1___ Can I help you?

_____ Will a driver's license do?

_____ Do you take credit cards?

Conversation B

_____ Do you have your receipt?

___1___ Can I help you?

_____ Yes, I do. Here it is.

_____ I'd rather get cash back.

_____ Okay. I can give you store credit for that amount.

_____ Can I speak to the manager, please?

_____ Yes, of course.

_____ Yes, I'd like to return this.

_____ I'm sorry but we only give store credit.

Conversation C

_____ Yes, of course. They come with a two year warranty.

___1___ Can I help you?

_____ That's correct. But you can also buy an extended warranty.

_____ Yes, can you tell me what the warranty is on the television sets?

_____ But it's only $5 a month. Really, it's a very good deal.

_____ Did you say two years?

_____ No thank you. I'll take the television set, but I'm not interested in an extended warranty.

_____ No thank you. I'm not interested in an extended warranty.

Conversation D

_____ And how would you like to pay for that?

_____ Yes, you have 30 days to return something.

_____ Yes, of course. But be sure to bring the receipt with you.

___1___ Can I help you?

_____ Is there a time limit?

_____ Yes. Can I bring this back if it doesn't fit my husband?

_____ Can I get cash back?

_____ That's good. I'll take this then.

_____ Yes, of course. You can make an exchange or a return.

_____ By cash.

All-Star 4 Study Guide for Post-Testing Copyright © McGraw-Hill

All-Star 4 Study Guide

Student Name _____   Date _____

Instructor Name _____

Demonstrate the ability to use the dictionary. Student Book page 90. LCP-E 83.09 . . . CASAS 7.4.5

USING A DICTIONARY

There is a lot of interesting and useful information in an English language learner's dictionary. In addition to finding the definition of a word, you can:

✓ learn how to pronounce a word.

✓ learn the part of speech of a word.

✓ learn the number of syllables in a word.

✓ learn irregular forms of nouns and verbs.

✓ find a synonym for a word.

✓ read sample sentences with the word.

✓ learn phrasal verbs such as "look into" and "find out."

✓ learn cultural information about the word.

Words in English often have more than one meaning. When you look up a word in a dictionary, make sure you choose the correct definition. The first definition is usually the most common, but it might not be the one you are looking for.

---

1 Read the dictionary definitions below and answer the questions.

bulk/ bûlk/ *n.* **1** large size: *Big animals, such as elephants and whales, have huge bulk.* **2** the most of s.t., (syn.) the majority: *The bulk of the students passed the exam.* **3 in bulk**: large amount: *You can save money by buying things in bulk.*

—*adj.* a bulk shipment: a large quantity: *The bulk shipment was 500 boxes of shoes.*

bulk•y/ bûlki / *adj.* -ier, -iest large and difficult to handle, (syn.) unwieldy: *A mattress is bulky for one person to carry.*

1. What is the most common meaning of the word *bulk*?

   _____

2. What is the superlative form of the word *bulky*?

   _____

3. What does *s.t.* mean? (Hint: *s.o.* means *someone*)

   _____

4. What is a synonym for one definition of *bulk*?

   _____

5. What is a synonym for the adjective *bulky*?

   _____

All-Star 4 Study Guide

Student Name _____   Date _____

Instructor Name _____

2 Read the dictionary definitions and the usage note and answer the questions below.

> **garage sale** *n.* a sale of used household items (old lamps, tables, etc.) inside or near a person's garage: *When my parents moved to a smaller house, they held a garage sale one weekend.*
>
> USAGE NOTE: Also known as yard sales, rummage sales, tag sales, or sidewalk sales, *garage sales* are popular in both cities and suburbs. Homeowners may post signs around their neighborhood to advertise a sale. People who live in apartments usually just put things out on the sidewalk and wait for passersby: *I need some bookshelves. Let's drive around the university area and look for a garage sale.*
>
> **yard sale** *n.* the sale of unwanted household items, such as old lamps, and tables, in a person's yard: *We bought a beautiful old table at a yard sale for $10! See:* garage sale, USAGE NOTE.

1. What is the difference between a yard sale and a garage sale?

2. This dictionary provides sample sentences in italics. Do the sample sentences help you to understand the meanings of the words?

3. What is the purpose of a usage note?

4. How helpful is this usage note to you?

3 Read the sentences and choose the correct definition for the word *yard* in each context. Circle 1 or 2.

> **yard** /yard/ *n.* **1** a length of three feet or 36 inches (0.91 meter): a yard of cloth **2** an area usually behind or in front of a house: *The children went outside to play in the yard.*

1. I spent an hour yesterday cleaning the yard.   1   2

2. I need 3 yards to make a new dress.   1   2

3. I found a yard of rope downstairs.   1   2

4. My new tie is a yard long.   1   2

5. My yard is about 20 yards wide.   1   2

All-Star 4 Study Guide

Student Name _____   Date _____

Instructor Name _____

See Student Book pages 92–93.

WRITING A LETTER OF COMPLAINT

Writing a letter of complaint is often the best way for a consumer to correct a problem. Be concise and direct in a letter of complaint and include the following information:

- the date and place of the purchase
- a description of the purchase
- a copy of the receipt

- an explanation of the problem
- the length of time you are willing to wait
- what you want

1 Read the written complaints and check (✓) the information each one provides.

	Email	Letter
1. the date the complaint was written	☐	☑
2. the date of the purchase	☐	☐
3. the recipient's name and address	☐	☐
4. the recipient's title	☐	☐
5. a description of the purchase	☐	☐
6. an explanation of the problem	☐	☐
7. what the writer wants	☐	☐
8. how long the writer will wait	☐	☐
9. the writer's name and address	☐	☐
10. a copy of the receipt	☐	☐

All-Star 4 Study Guide

Student Name _____   Date _____

Instructor Name _____

Write complex and compound sentences with correct terminology and punctuation. Workbook page 98. LCP-E 83.16

A Unscramble the questions below. Then use the picture to answer them.

1. have / do / you / financing

   Customer: _____

   Salesperson: _____

2. here / sell / can / my car / for cash / I

   Customer: _____

   Salesperson: _____

3. for sale / have / do you / any trucks

   Customer: _____

   Salesperson: _____

4. any / your cars / a warranty / do / come with / of

   Customer: _____

   Salesperson: _____

All-Star 4 Study Guide for Post-Testing Copyright © McGraw-Hill

All-Star 4 Study Guide

Student Name _____   Date _____

Instructor Name _____

A Add the correct tag to each statement on the right. Write the tag on the line.

1. He didn't like it, _____?   a. can she
2. That was a profitable business, _____?   b. isn't it
3. He speaks Spanish very well, _____?   c. was it
4. That's the end of the movie, _____?   d. do they
5. Shoes cost a lot, _____?   e. is it
6. It wasn't very cold yesterday, _____?   f. did he
7. She can't sing very well, _____?   g. didn't he
8. Clothes from thrift stores don't cost a lot, _____?   h. wasn't it
9. That dress isn't very pretty, _____?   i. don't they
10. He certainly left in a hurry, _____?   j. doesn't he

B Add tag questions to complete the conversations.

1. A: This is a great movie, _____?
   B: It sure is. The beginning was scary though, _____?
   A: Absolutely. I couldn't believe it.

2. A: This grapefruit is really sour, _____?
   B: It sure is.

3. A: There certainly wasn't much to eat at the party, _____?
   B: No, there wasn't. I'm still hungry.

4. A: She couldn't sing very well tonight, _____?
   B: No, she couldn't. She's usually much better.

5. A: He hit the floor hard, _____?
   B: He certainly did. I can't believe he didn't break any bones.

6. A: She spoke very well, _____?
   B: Yes, she did. She always does.

Use verbs:- - tag questions/answers. Workbook page 90. LCP-E 84.01 . . . BEST *Plus*

All-Star 4 Study Guide

Student Name _____   Date _____

Instructor Name _____

WINDOW ON PRONUNCIATION 🎧
Intonation in Tag Questions

 Read the information.

When tag questions are used to give an opinion or confirm something, they have rising and then falling intonation. When tag questions are used like a *yes/no* question, they have rising intonation.

 Listen to the questions. Then listen and repeat.

Question	Confirmation	Yes/No
1. That's a really good price, isn't it?	❏	❏
2. You didn't bring your credit card, did you?	❏	❏
3. We paid that bill last month, didn't we?	❏	❏
4. They can't cancel our subscription without notice, can they?	❏	❏
5. These cookies aren't very fresh, are they?	❏	❏

 Listen to the questions again and check the appropriate box.

D Write two tag questions below and ask a classmate your questions.

1. _____

2. _____

All-Star 4 Study Guide

Student Name _____ Date _____

Instructor Name _____

See Workbook page 115.

A Read the questions in the chart below and write your guesses in column 2.

1 Questions	2 My guesses before reading the text	3 Answers from the text
a) Twenty-five-year-old Sandra is a cashier in a large store. Last week her boss asked her to help unpack boxes in the storeroom. Sandra doesn't think she should have to do this because it's not in her job description. Is she right?		
b) Fong works from Wednesday through Sunday. A friend told him that he should get extra pay when he works on the weekend. Is his friend correct?		
c) Selena earns $10.00 an hour and last week she worked for 45 hours. How much money should her employer pay her for the week?		
d) Twelve-year-old Jesse wants to earn some money so she can take dance lessons. What types of work can she do?		
e) Sixteen-year-old Andy is trying to save money for college. What types of jobs can he do?		

Now read the information on Workbook page 115 and look for the answers to the questions in Activity A. Then write the answers in column 3 of the chart.

Demonstrate understanding of worker's rights (compensation, unionization, right to work). Workbook page 114. LCP-E 70.04 . . . CASAS 4.2.2

All-Star 4 Study Guide

Student Name _____   Date _____

Instructor Name _____

A Unscramble the words to write sentences.

1. the Marriage License Division / reached / have / you

_____

2. required / premarital / are / physicals / not

_____

3. it is issued / valid / is / for 60 days thereafter / the marriage license / on the day / and

_____

_____

4. $50 / the cost / in cash / is

_____

5. processed / applications / are / from 8:30 to 4:00

_____

6. to complete / take / 45 minutes / approximately / it will / the application process

_____

_____

7. on the application / your social security number / have / must / you

_____

8. bring / your date of birth / you must / a valid driver's license / or photo ID / with

_____

B Complete the telephone conversation with information from Activity A.

1. A. Do I need to have a physical exam before I can get a marriage license?

   B. _____

2. A. How long will it take to get the license?

   B. _____

3. A. So do you think I will be finished in half an hour?

   B. _____

All-Star 4 Study Guide

Student Name _____   Date _____

Instructor Name _____

Discuss U.S. driving responsibilities and driver's license exam with emphasis on auto insurance (driver's license, traffic regulations, insurance, seat belts, child safety restraints). Workbook page 116. LCP-E 77.02 . . . CASAS 1.9.1, 1.9.2, 1.9.8, 2.2.1, 2.2.2

DIRECTIONS: Read the article to answer the next 5 questions. Use the Answer Sheet.

Speed Laws

In this state, residential and business zones are 30 miles per hour unless otherwise posted. School zones are 15 miles per hour unless otherwise posted. This speed limit is observed 30 minutes before to 30 minutes after school is in session.

Maximum safe speed on highways is 55 miles per hour. Certain limited access highways may have a posted limit of 65 or 70 mph in specific areas. However, unless posted, you should observe a speed limit of no more than 55 mph.

Your maximum safe driving speed is always determined by the road and weather conditions. The posted speed limit is the maximum speed that is ever allowed, and it may not be appropriate for all conditions. You can get a speeding ticket for driving at the posted limit if conditions are unsafe, for example in snow, rain, or ice.

Fines will be doubled if there are constructions workers in a work zone, or if children are present in a school zone.

1. When should you drive <u>below</u> the speed limit?
   A. when it is snowing
   B. when the road is in bad condition
   C. when you can't see
   D. all of the above

2. What is the usual speed limit on highways?
   A. 65
   B. 70
   C. 55
   D. 35

3. When do you have to pay twice as much in fines?
   A. when workers or children are present in the zone
   B. when you go twice the speed limit
   C. when the conditions are unsafe
   D. when you are on the highway

4. What is the speed limit in residential zones?
   A. 55 mph
   B. 30 mph
   C. 15 mph
   D. 60 mph

5. Under what condition do you have to drive 15 mph in a school zone?
   A. in bad weather
   B. at night
   C. 30 minutes before school to 30 minutes after school is over
   D. all the time

ANSWER SHEET

1 Ⓐ Ⓑ Ⓒ Ⓓ
2 Ⓐ Ⓑ Ⓒ Ⓓ
3 Ⓐ Ⓑ Ⓒ Ⓓ
4 Ⓐ Ⓑ Ⓒ Ⓓ
5 Ⓐ Ⓑ Ⓒ Ⓓ
6 Ⓐ Ⓑ Ⓒ Ⓓ
7 Ⓐ Ⓑ Ⓒ Ⓓ
8 Ⓐ Ⓑ Ⓒ Ⓓ
9 Ⓐ Ⓑ Ⓒ Ⓓ
10 Ⓐ Ⓑ Ⓒ Ⓓ

All-Star 4 Study Guide

Student Name _____   Date _____

Instructor Name _____

Demonstrate appropriate response when stopped by law enforcement officers. Workbook page 108. LCP-E 77.03 . . . CASAS 1.9.7, 5.3.5

A Read the questions in the chart below and write your guesses in column 2.

1 Questions	2 My guesses before reading the text	3 Answers from the text
a) What rights do people have when they are arrested?		
b) How should a person behave when arrested?		
c) What can people do if they can't afford to pay a lawyer?		

B Read the information below and look for answers to the questions in Activity A. Write the answers in column 3 of the chart.

What You Should Do if You're Arrested

Act Thoughtfully

Don't argue with the arresting officer. Keep your hands visible and don't move suddenly. What you say and do can be used against you, so be respectful and polite. Stay calm. If the arrest is a mistake, you can sort it out later. The important thing is to stay in control.

Know Your Rights

Everyone has rights when they are arrested. The arresting officer should read you your rights. These rights include the right to remain silent and the right to a lawyer. You do not have to say anything until you are represented by an attorney. You should be able to make a phone call.

Get a Lawyer

It's always wise to have legal representation when you have been arrested. Your attorney can advise you on what you should do. If you can't afford your own attorney, a judge will appoint one for you that will provide services for free. Legal aid services also provide low-cost representation to clients with little money.

All-Star 4 Study Guide

Student Name _____   Date _____

Instructor Name _____

See Workbook page 108.

C Check (✓) *True* or *False*.

	True	False
1. Only citizens have rights when they are arrested.	☐	☐
2. You should protest to the officer if you think the arrest is unfair.	☐	☐
3. You must answer police questions when arrested.	☐	☐
4. If you don't have any money, you can get a lawyer for free.	☐	☐
5. Only guilty people need lawyers.	☐	☐
6. Legal aid services are often available at little or no cost.	☐	☐

D Answer the following questions.

1. Why do you think some people don't call a lawyer when they are arrested?

   _____

   _____

2. What mistakes do you think people might make when they are stopped by the police?

   _____

   _____

3. Why do you think it is important to move slowly and keep your hands visible?

   _____

   _____

Demonstrate appropriate response when stopped by law enforcement officers. Workbook page 109. LCP-E 77.03 . . . CASAS 1.9.7, 5.3.5

All-Star 4 Study Guide

Student Name _____   Date _____

Instructor Name _____

1 Warm Up

Work with your classmates to answer the questions below.

1. What are the biggest problems in your neighborhood?
2. How safe is your neighborhood?
3. What can individuals do to make their neighborhoods safer?

2 Read and Respond

Read the information below and answer the questions.

Making Changes

Neighborhood Watch is an organization of citizens in a neighborhood. The members of a Neighborhood Watch program work with the police to protect their community. Neighborhood Watch members watch for unusual activity in their neighborhood and report it to the police.

It's a story of hard work and pride. In 1975, Trong Nguyen arrived in Chicago from Vietnam. He and his family were fleeing the last days of war.

But the "Uptown" area the refugees moved into seemed like another war zone. The streets were filled with muggers, drug addicts, and other dangerous people. It was not a good place for families with children.

But people like Trong Nguyen were determined to save the neighborhood. They worked with police and other community leaders. Groups were formed to watch for trouble. Before long, much of the crime stopped.

Meanwhile, Trong opened a small restaurant. Other people from Laos, Cambodia, and Vietnam started businesses in stores that had been empty. Soon, the addicts and gangs disappeared.

Today, Chicago's "Uptown" is no longer a dangerous, run down area, thanks to Trong and others. People from all over the city come to visit its stores and restaurants. It's a special place.

Source: *U.S. Express*, Scholastic, Inc.

QUESTIONS

1. Why wasn't Trong's neighborhood in Chicago a good place to live?
2. What did Trong do to change his neighborhood?
3. What is Trong's neighborhood like now?
4. Do you think the Neighborhood Watch program is a good idea? Why or why not?

BEST *Plus:* Do you think violence on television can promote violent behavior? Why?

All-Star 4 Study Guide

Student Name _____ **Date** _____

Instructor Name _____

See Student book pages 94–95.

THINGS TO DO

1 Warm Up

Work with your classmates to answer the questions below.

1. Have you ever seen a courtroom in real life or in a movie? Describe what happened.
2. What are the people in this courtroom doing?

2 Identify

Who in this courtroom does each thing below? Write your guesses. Then compare ideas with a classmate. Find the words in the glossary on page 171 to check your answers.

_____ decides if the defendant is guilty or not guilty

_____ records what people say

_____ is in charge of the courtroom

_____ keeps peace in the courtroom

_____ tries to prove the **defendant** is not guilty

_____ tries to show the defendant is guilty

_____ describes what he or she saw

3 Put in Sequence

Read the journal entries on page 94 and put the events below in order from first (1) to last (8).

_____ The **jury** went into a special room.

_____ She went to court for the first time.

_____ She became a member of the jury.

_____ A **judge** and two lawyers interviewed her.

_____ She received a summons for jury duty in her mailbox.

_____ She received a check from the court.

_____ The jury made a decision.

_____ She listened to the testimony of many **witnesses**.

Compare ideas with a classmate. Then take turns telling the story in your own words.

Demonstrate understanding of trial by jury and other elements in a U.S. court of law (judge, jury, lawyers, and legal assistance). Student Book page 94. LCP-E 80.04 . . . CASAS 5.1.4, 5.3.3, 5.5.3, 5.5.6, 5.6.3

All-Star 4 Study Guide

Student Name _____   Date _____

Instructor Name _____

Develop awareness of acceptable/unacceptable parenting and disciplinary practices. *BEST Plus: Describe whether or not parental involvement in a child's education helps children.* Workbook page 112. LCP-E 82.03...CASAS 3.5.7 ... *BEST Plus*

A Read questions 1 to 3. Then read the information below and answer the questions.

1. How did the boy misbehave?

_____

2. How did his parents punish him?

_____

3. Why do the parents now have a record of suspected child abuse?

_____

QUESTION

My family came from India five years ago. My son's friends at school were bad boys who told him to miss school and stay out late. My husband and I grew tired of this behavior, and locked our son in his room for two days. His teacher learned about his punishment and reported us for child abuse. Someone came to our house to investigate. Even though the investigation has ended, we still have a record of suspected[1] child abuse. Why did this happen?

ANSWER

American laws give parents a lot of freedom on how to discipline their children. But the laws also protect children if the authorities believe that the discipline becomes dangerous. The government strictly enforces these laws against child abuse and child neglect[2]. These laws are meant to protect the safety of children, even if the parents do not mean to hurt the children. You need to understand how the American laws affect how you raise your children, and you may have to learn new ways to discipline your children.

The U.S. laws are based on the views of the general American society, which may be different from your own views. It does not matter how people in your home country use discipline. You will be judged by the customs of America and not by your own personal religious or cultural beliefs. Your best protection is to know the law. Once a child abuse report is made, the process can take weeks, months, or even years to end. You may have to go to court. The government can even take your children away from your home *before* you go to court.

_____
[1] suspected: not yet proven
[2] neglect: failure to provide proper care

From *Understanding the Laws On How You Can Discipline Your Children* by Lydia Fan, The Coalition for Asian American Children and Families, January 2002. Reprinted by permission.

BEST *Plus:* Do you think a parent should be involved in a child's education? Why?

All-Star 4 Study Guide for Post-Testing Copyright © McGraw-Hill

All-Star 4 Study Guide

Student Name _____   Date _____

Instructor Name _____

See Workbook page 112.

B Read the sentences and check (✓) *True* or *False*.

	True	False
1. U.S. laws allow parents to use any form of discipline.	☐	☐
2. The government rarely enforces laws against child abuse.	☐	☐
3. A teacher can report a suspected case of child abuse.	☐	☐
4. The way your parents disciplined you may not be legal in the U.S.	☐	☐
5. You may have to go to court if you are accused of child neglect.	☐	☐

C There are many forms of child abuse and child neglect. Group these examples in the chart below.

burning   shaking

failing to send to school   shaming

failing to take to the doctor   slapping

not feeding properly   name calling

kicking   not using a child seat for a baby in a car

Physical Abuse	Emotional Abuse	Neglect

Develop awareness of acceptable/unacceptable parenting and disciplinary practices. *BEST Plus: Describe whether or not parental involvement in a child's education helps children.* Workbook page 113. LCP-E 82.03…CASAS 3.5.7 … BEST *Plus*

BEST *Plus:* Do you think a parent should be involved in a child's education? Why?

Unit 6   **73**

All-Star 4 Study Guide

Student Name _____   Date _____

Instructor Name _____

Paraphrase passages, words, or ideas in conversations. Workbook page 107. LCP-E 83.02

C Paraphrase the following statements.

1. If you are between the ages of 18 and 21, you must present a valid driver's license or photo ID, and a certified birth certificate.

   _____

   _____

2. You must complete driver's education before you can take the test to get a learner's permit.

   _____

   _____

3. A permit is required to deposit garbage at the county dump site.

   _____

4. Recyclables, such as glass bottles and aluminum containers, may be brought in to the recycling center without a permit and are free of charge as long as they are kept separate from trash.

   _____

   _____

   _____

All-Star 4 Study Guide for Post-Testing. Copyright © McGraw-Hill

All-Star 4 Study Guide

Student Name _____   Date _____

Instructor Name _____

Interpret statistical information from diagrams, tables, graphs, charts, and schedules. Workbook page 105. LCP-E 83.13 . . . . CASAS 6.6.5

C Look at the bar graph. Circle the correct answers to the questions below.

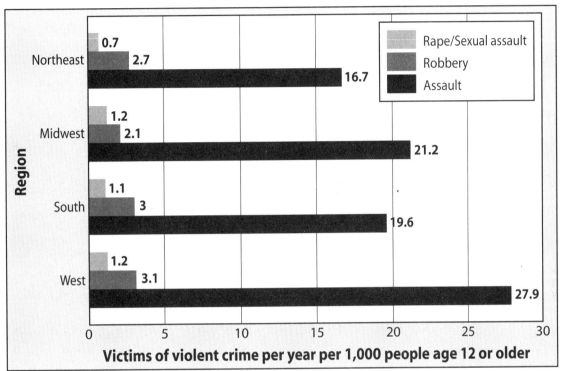

Legend:
- Rape/Sexual assault
- Robbery
- Assault

Northeast: 0.7 / 2.7 / 16.7
Midwest: 1.2 / 2.1 / 21.2
South: 1.1 / 3 / 19.6
West: 1.2 / 3.1 / 27.9

Region (y-axis)

Victims of violent crime per year per 1,000 people age 12 or older (x-axis: 0, 5, 10, 15, 20, 25, 30)

Source: http://www.ojp.usdoj.gov/

1. In which region of the United States is the rate of assault the greatest?
   A. the Northeast   C. the South
   B. the Midwest   D. the West

2. Where is there the lowest incidence of robberies?
   A. the Northeast   C. the South
   B. the Midwest   D. the West

3. Which region has the fewest rapes or sexual assaults?
   A. the Northeast   C. the South
   B. the Midwest   D. the West

4. Which region is the safest overall in terms of these violent crimes?
   A. the Northeast   C. the South
   B. the Midwest   D. the West

5. Which region is the most dangerous?
   A. the Northeast   C. the South
   B. the Midwest   D. the West

Unit 6   **75**

All-Star 4 Study Guide

Student Name _____   Date _____

Instructor Name _____

Write a paragraph focusing on one topic (narration, definition, description, cause and effect). Student Book page 109. LCP-E 83.15

3 Read the article and take notes in the chart below. Then use your notes to summarize the article.

Violence on TV

Do you think it is **no big deal** if somebody gets killed on TV? Is it funny to you if people on TV hit each other? If so, maybe you are watching too much violence on TV.

Shows with violence should tell the truth, but often they do not. In real life, violence hurts. Flattened animals and people don't become round again and walk away. Bad guys are not always ugly so that you can tell right away who they are. Bad guys are not always caught. Bad guys do not always break down when police question them.

If you watch too many violent shows, you may start thinking that violence is more common and less serious than it is. It may seem to you that bad guys are on every corner and that you will have to use violence to defend yourself.

Violence *is* a part of life, but it is not a part of life to take lightly. Violence usually creates problems instead of solving them, and the problems it creates are very tough to solve. That is why, in real life, most people try hard to avoid ever using violence.

What TV puts in your brain is likely to stay there. Keep that in mind when you watch it.

Source: *The Macmillan Book of Fascinating Facts,* by Ann Elwood and Carol Madigan

Cause *watching too many violent shows on TV*	→	Effects

Summary:

_____

_____

_____

_____

_____

_____

All-Star 4 Study Guide

C Read the letter. Write *who, that, which,* or X (if no pronoun is needed) on the lines.

Dear Linda,

You'll never believe what happened! Remember I told you about the guy Rick _____ (1) works at the desk next to me? Well, he asked me to go to a nightclub _____ (2) just opened a week ago. Lots of people _____ (3) I know from work went too. Anyway, we had been there about an hour when we decided to leave to get something to eat. We wanted to go to a new restaurant downtown _____ (4) opened a few months ago. We went to the parking garage, but Rick's truck wasn't there! We spoke to the man _____ (5) was working there and he said that he saw a blue pick-up truck leave thirty minutes earlier. Rick used a cell phone _____ (6) another person in the garage had to call 911. Two police officers came and Rick _____ (7) filed a report with them. By this time it was getting late and I wanted to go home. We asked the police about transportation, but they said the bus _____ (8) goes by there only operates until 9:00 P.M. So we had to take a taxi, _____ (9) was expensive.

The next day Rick got a call from one of the police officers _____ (10) said she had found his truck. You'll never believe where she found it—in the parking garage. We were sure we had parked on the 4th floor, but I guess we had actually parked on the 5th floor. Rick was so embarrassed _____ (11) he didn't talk to me at all the next week. I finally spoke with him this week and _____ (12) we made plans to go out again. This time I'm driving!

—Mila

D Answer the questions about you. Use adjective clauses in your answer.

1. What person has influenced you the most?

_____

_____

2. What do you think is the most serious public safety problem?

_____

_____

3. What do you think contributes to crime?

_____

_____

Write complex and compound sentences with correct terminology and punctuation. Workbook page 111. LCP-E 83.16

All-Star 4 Study Guide for Post-Testing Copyright © McGraw-Hill

All-Star 4 Study Guide

Student Name _____   Date _____

Instructor Name _____

Describe personal career goals, interests, and review jobs including LPN, typist. Workbook page 133. LCP-E 69.01 . . . CASAS 4.1.4, 4.1.8, 4.4.5, 7.1.1

C What advice would you give to each of these people?

1. Anita, a high school student, is interested in both computers and nursing. What career planning advice could you give her? Why?

   Your advice:

2. Pépé would like to have a job working with people. He's especially interested in working in sales. What career planning advice could you give him? Why?

   Your advice:

TAKE IT ONLINE: Use your favorite search engine to find the U.S. Department of Labor, Bureau of Labor Statistics. On the Bureau of Labor Statistics website, find a chart with information that is interesting to you. List 3 interesting things you learned from the chart.

1. _____

2. _____

3. _____

All-Star 4 Study Guide for Post-Testing Copyright © McGraw-Hill

All-Star 4 Study Guide

Student Name _____   Date _____

Instructor Name _____

Complete the sample form with your information.

APPLICATION FOR EMPLOYMENT

PERSONAL INFORMATION:

Date _____   Available Start Date _____

☐ Full Time   ☐ Part Time   ☐ Temporary   Referral Source _____

Name _____   Phone _____

Street Address _____

City/State/Zip _____   SSN _____

EDUCATION:

Schools Attended	# of Years	Year Grad	Degree

EMPLOYMENT/WORK EXPERIENCE:

Start with your present or most recent position. (Attach another sheet of paper for additional work experience.)

Employer	Job Title
Supervisor	Phone
Describe Duties/Responsibilities/Accomplishments	Reason for Leaving
Dates of Employment (Month/Year) From:	To:

Employer	Job Title
Supervisor	Phone
Describe Duties/Responsibilities/Accomplishments	Reason for Leaving
Dates of Employment (Month/Year) From:	To:

BUSINESS REFERENCE:

Please provide contact information for one or more business references. (Attach another sheet of paper for additional references.)

Name _____   Company _____

Position _____   Phone _____

SPECIAL SKILLS:

Describe any skills or qualifications you have for this work.

_____

Complete job applications and write a résumé and cover letter. Student Book page 191. LCP-E 69.03 . . . CASAS 4.1.2

All-Star 4 Study Guide for Post-Testing Copyright © McGraw-Hill

All-Star 4 Study Guide

Student Name _____   Date _____

Instructor Name _____

See Student Book page 117.

Demonstrate standards of behavior for job interview; ask and answer questions during a job interview; write a thank you note; conduct a follow-up call after a simulated job interview. *BEST Plus: Describe emotions or feelings about interviews.* Student Book page 116. LCP-E 69.04. . . CASAS 4.1.5, 4.4.1, 4.4.3, 4.6.2. . .BEST *Plus*

THINGS TO DO

1 Warm Up

Work with your classmates to answer the questions below.

1. When was the last time you interviewed for a job? How did it go?
2. What should and shouldn't you do at a job interview?
3. What are 5 things you know about Roberta from her job application on page 117?

2 Listen for Specific Information 🎧

Listen to Roberta's interview and add the missing information to her job application on page 117.

3 Listen and Evaluate 🎧

Read the questions below. Then look at the pictures and listen to the interview again. Check (✓) your answers.

Do you think Roberta _____?	Yes, very.	Yes.	No.
1. was dressed appropriately	☐	☐	☐
2. was prepared for the interview	☐	☐	☐
3. spoke clearly	☐	☐	☐
4. was businesslike	☐	☐	☐
5. was polite	☐	☐	☐
6. had a friendly tone of voice	☐	☐	☐
7. had a positive attitude	☐	☐	☐

Now listen to Richard's interview. On another piece of paper, answer questions 1–7 about him. Then compare each interview.

Roberta submits her résumé.

Richard completes his application.

BEST *Plus:* Interviews can make a person very nervous. How do you usually feel during a job interview?

All-Star 4 Study Guide

Student Name _____   Date _____

Instructor Name _____

Demonstrate understanding of job specifications, policies, standards, benefits, W2 and W4 forms. Complete sample W4 form; wages, deductions, and timekeeping forms. Student Book page 123. LCP-E 69.05 . . . CASAS 4.1.1, 4.2.1, 4.2.3, 4.4.4

3 Apply

Below is a list of family-friendly job benefits that some companies offer. Number them in importance to you from most important (1) to least important (10).

a. _____ Paid vacation of two weeks or more

b. _____ Health and dental insurance for all family members

c. _____ Tuition assistance

d. _____ Merchandise discount: the ability to buy the company's products at a discount.

e. _____ Flexible schedules: the ability to adjust work schedules to fit school or child-care schedules

f. _____ Telecommuting: the ability to work from home, when appropriate

g. _____ On-site day care

h. _____ Company help in finding child care

i. _____ Sixteen weeks of unpaid leave to take care of a sick family member, give birth, or adopt a child

j. _____ Job sharing: two half-time employees work to meet the demands of one full-time position

---

WINDOW ON MATH
Computing Averages

 Read the information.

You can find the average of a set of numbers by adding all the numbers and dividing by the number in the sample.

Daily classroom attendance for the week of January 8th:

Mon.		Tues.		Wed.		Thurs.		Fri.
17	+	15	+	13	+	14	+	16

Average daily attendance
$$17 + 15 + 13 + 14 + 16 = 75 \div 5 \ (\text{\# of days}) = 15$$

 Compute the average.

1. Six people work at Speedy Copy. Their hourly wages are as follows: Jim ($10), Cindy ($12), Ken ($11), Ivan ($15), Lucy ($13) and Chang ($14). What is the average hourly pay at Speedy Copy? _____

2. In one department at SouthWood, there are 8 full-time employees. Look at the number of sick days taken in one year by each employee. What is the average number of sick days taken by employees in that department?

Ming	7	Mahmoud	2
Park	3	Thomas	6
Sanders	2	Grant	1
Oliveira	5	Lopez	8

All-Star 4 Study Guide

Student Name _____   **Date** _____

Instructor Name _____

See Student Book page 113.

Demonstrate understanding of U.S. work ethic (appropriate behavior, attire, attitudes, and social interactions that affect job performance). Student Book page 112. LCP-E 70.01 . . . CASAS 4.2.4, 4.4.1, 4.4.6 . . . BEST *Plus*

THINGS TO DO

1 Warm Up

Work with your classmates to answer these questions.

1. What are the characteristics of a good job?
2. Would you like to work in the store in the picture? Why or why not?
3. What do you see employees in the picture doing?

2 Analyze

Study the picture and read the work rules. Then answer the questions below.

1. Which work rule is the most serious to break?
2. What are 5 other types of inappropriate work place behavior?
3. Find 5 people in the picture who are breaking a work rule. What are they doing?
4. Who in the picture do you think is in charge? Why?

3 Solve Problems

Work with a partner to discuss the situations below. Then share ideas with your classmates.

1. Simon is a new employee at the company and Joe, a coworker, is training him. Joe spends a lot of time on the job loafing. Simon doesn't like to loaf on the job, but Joe is training him. What should Simon do?
2. Nancy frequently makes lengthy personal calls during work hours. Jane, her coworker, can hear Nancy talking and laughing on the phone and it makes it hard for Jane to work. What should Jane do?

All-Star 4 Study Guide

Student Name _____   Date _____

Instructor Name _____

Read the job descriptions to answer the questions.

ADMINISTRATIVE ASSISTANT

Responsibilities:
- Assist department chair
- Update classes in mainframe computer
- Maintain student records
- Submit end-of-term forms, including grades and attendance records
- Assist instructors with forms

Skills:
Can use office software; previous experience in office setting
Salary: $12 an hour

FINANCIAL AID COUNSELOR

Responsibilities:
- Meet with and counsel students on financial aid process
- Review financial aid applications
- Maintain student financial aid records in mainframe computer
- Oversee work-study positions as needed

Skills:
B.A. required in business, education, or counseling; 2 years experience in higher ed. setting
Salary: $30,000 annually

CASHIER

Responsibilities:
- Handle tuition payments, including cash, check, or credit payments
- Maintain records
- Handle customer questions and concerns
- Count and balance money, prepare deposits

Skills:
1 year experience as cashier
Salary: $10 an hour

REGISTRAR

Responsibilities:
- Maintain student registration records
- Use computer registration system
- Handle student questions, concerns, complaints
- Provide excellent service

Skills:
B.A. in administration required, M.A. preferred, plus 3 years experience in educational setting
Salary: $35,000+

1. Which job is the highest paying?
   A. Administrative assistant
   B. Cashier
   C. Financial aid counselor
   D. Registrar

2. Which job has the lowest salary?
   A. Administrative assistant
   B. Cashier
   C. Financial aid counselor
   D. Registrar

3. Which job does not require computer use?
   A. Administrative assistant
   B. Cashier
   C. Financial aid counselor
   D. Registrar

4. Which job requires the most experience?
   A. Administrative assistant
   B. Cashier
   C. Financial aid counselor
   D. Registrar

5. Which job asks for the most education?
   A. Administrative assistant
   B. Cashier
   C. Financial aid counselor
   D. Registrar

Compare and contrast job tasks, responsibilities, and levels of training. Workbook page 136. LCP-E 70.03 … CASAS 7.2.3

All-Star 4 Study Guide for Post-Testing Copyright © McGraw Hill

All-Star 4 Study Guide

Student Name _____   Date _____

Instructor Name _____

See Student Book pages 118–119.

Demonstrate an understanding of work performance evaluations and their impact on promotions. Student Book page 118. LCP-E 71.02

THINGS TO DO

1 Warm Up

Work with your classmates to answer the questions below.

1. What are 5 characteristics of the ideal employee and the ideal employer? List your ideas in a chart like the one below. Then share ideas with your classmates.

The ideal employee	The ideal employer
is always on time	is fair

2. If you want to get a job promotion, what should you do? What shouldn't you do?

2 Read and Respond

Read the employee performance evaluation on page 119 and answer the questions below.

1. What do you know about Sarah Wang from her performance evaluation?
2. What are Sarah's greatest strengths on the job?
3. What is Sarah's greatest weakness on the job?
4. What are 3 things Sarah could do to improve her job performance?

3 Make Inferences

Match each comment below to one or more possible inferences.

Comments	Inferences
1. Petra completes her work on time. She _c, e, h_	a. is polite
2. Max prepares deposits accurately. He _____.	b. is creative
3. Tim often comes in early to work. He _____.	c. is dependable
4. Paul helped to train 3 new employees. He _____.	d. is punctual
5. Mei is very friendly with everyone. She _____.	e. is productive
6. Yoshiko does what needs to be done. She _____.	f. is cooperative
7. Hiro always has wonderful new ideas. He _____.	g. shows initiative
8. Patricia **delivers** her work on time. She _____.	h. has good job skills
9. Tony shows respect to everyone. He _____.	i. works independently
	j. other: _____

All-Star 4 Study Guide

Student Name _____   Date _____

Instructor Name _____

C Read this story by Aesop and underline the words that help you follow the sequence of events.

The Lion and the Mouse

ONCE when a Lion was asleep a little Mouse began running up and down upon him; this soon wakened the Lion, who placed his huge paw upon him, and opened his big jaws to swallow him. "Pardon, O King," cried the little Mouse: "forgive me this time, I shall never forget it: who knows but what I may be able to do you a turn some of these days?" The Lion was so tickled at the idea of the Mouse being able to help him, that he lifted up his paw and let him go. Some time after the Lion was caught in a trap, and the hunters, who desired to carry him alive to the King, tied him to a tree while they went in search of a wagon to carry him on. Just then the little

 Mouse happened to pass by, and seeing the sad plight in which the Lion was, went up to him and soon gnawed away the ropes that bound the King of the Beasts. "Was I not right?" said the little Mouse.

"Little friends may prove great friends."

D Rewrite the story in your own words.

_____
_____
_____
_____
_____
_____
_____
_____
_____
_____
_____

Paraphrase passages, words, or ideas in conversations. Workbook page 139. LCP-E 83.02

All-Star 4 Study Guide

Student Name _____ Date _____

Instructor Name _____

C Add a prefix (*dis, il, im, in, un*) to the following words to change the meaning from positive to negative.

_____ legal	_____ literate	_____ legible
_____ proper	_____ possible	_____ mature
_____ appropriate	_____ correct	_____ capable
_____ necessary	_____ acceptable	_____ usual
_____ orderly	_____ connect	_____ agree

D Complete the questions with words from Activity C. Answers can vary.

1. What do you consider _____ behavior at work?

2. Where is it _____ to wear pajamas?

3. How does your teacher react when you give an _____ answer?

4. What kinds of discrimination are _____ in the workplace according to the Equal Employment Opportunity Commission?

5. What should you do if you _____ with something your supervisor asks you to do?

E Answer the questions in Activity D.

1. _____

2. _____

3. _____

4. _____

5. _____

Utilize new vocabulary by context. Workbook page 123. LCP-E 83.06

All-Star 4 Study Guide

Student Name _____   Date _____

Instructor Name _____

See Student Book page 127.

Recognize sequence of events in a reading passage. Student Book page 126. LCP-E 83.07

IDENTIFYING A SEQUENCE OF EVENTS

When you are reading about a sequence of events, it's important to keep track of what happened and in what order. Below are some words that can help you follow a sequence of events.

after	before	later	previously
after that	first	meanwhile	today
afterwards	in + (year) then	now	

1 Read the paragraph below. Circle the words that help you follow the sequence of events.

Working part-time can be a good way to get your foot in the door, says Nancy Lin. Her (first) job was as a part-time sales associate with Mill's Hardware at their store in Springvale. Meanwhile, she continued studying full time to get her degree. Immediately after graduating, she began working full time at the store. Soon after that she became an assistant store manager, and today she is a successful general manager of the Mill's store in San Bernardo. Who knows what's next, but before she started college, Nancy wasn't quite sure what kind of job she would have. She's happy with the outcome.

2 Read about Franklin Chang-Diaz on page 127. List some of the important events in his life in the boxes below. Sequence them from the beginning.

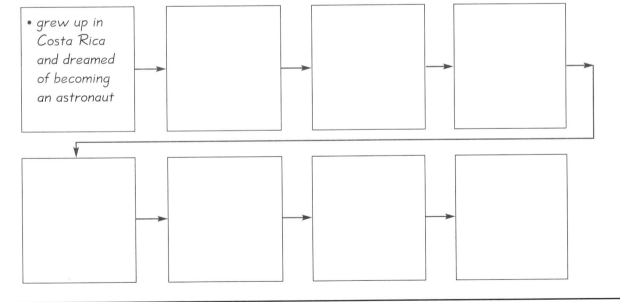

• grew up in Costa Rica and dreamed of becoming an astronaut

All-Star 4 Study Guide

Student Name _____   Date _____

Instructor Name _____

Interpret statistical information from diagrams, tables, graphs, charts, and schedules. Workbook page 132. LCP-E 83.13 . . . . CASAS 6.6.5

A Study the charts and read the sentences below. Check (✓) *True* or *False*.

	True	False
1. These charts show what might happen in the workforce in the future.	☐	☐
2. These charts give information about the workforce for the next twenty years.	☐	☐
3. Chart 1 says that by 2012 there might be a need for about 600,000 more registered nurses in the workforce.	☐	☐
4. According to Chart 2, there will be about 25,000 fewer positions for farmers and ranchers in the U.S. workforce by 2012.	☐	☐
5. According to Chart 2, the need for farmers and ranchers will decrease more than the need for sewing machine operators.	☐	☐

Chart 1:

Occupations with the largest numerical increases in employment, projected 2002–2012

- Registered nurses
- Postsecondary teachers
- Retail salespersons
- Customer service representatives
- Combined food preparation and serving workers, including fast food
- Cashiers, except gaming
- Janitors and cleaners, except maids and housekeeping cleaners
- General and operations managers
- Waiters and waitresses
- Nursing aides, orderlies, and attendants
- Truck drivers, heavy and tractor-trailer
- Receptionists and information clerks
- Security guards
- Office clerks, general
- Teacher assistants
- Sales representatives, wholesale and manufacturing, except technical and scientific products
- Home health aides
- Personal and home care aides
- Truck drivers, light or delivery services
- Landscaping and groundskeeping workers

0   100   200   300   400   500   600   700
Increase (in thousands)

Chart 2:

Job declines in occupations with the largest numerical decreases in employment, projected 2002–2012

- Farmers and ranchers
- Sewing machine operators
- Word processors and typists
- Stock clerks and order fillers
- Secretaries, except legal, medical and executive
- Electrical and electronic equipment assemblers
- Computer operators
- Telephone operators
- Postal Service mail sorters, processors, processing machine operators
- Loan interviewers and clerks
- Data-entry keyers
- Telemarketers
- Textile knitting and weaving machine operators, and tenders
- Textile winding, twisting, and drawing out machine setters, operators, and tenders
- Team assemblers
- Order clerks
- Door-to-door sales workers, news vendors, and related workers
- Travel agents
- Brokerage clerks
- Eligibility interviewers, government programs

−250   −200   −150   −100   −50   0
Decrease (in thousands)

Source: www.bls.gov

All-Star 4 Study Guide

Student Name _____   Date _____

Instructor Name _____

See Workbook page 132.

Interpret statistical information from diagrams, tables, graphs, charts, and schedules. Workbook page 133. LCP-E 83.13 . . . . CASAS 6.6.5

B Use the charts on page 132 to answer the questions below. Circle your answers.

1. Which of these occupations will probably employ more people in the future than today?

   A. travel agents   B. home health aides   C. telemarketers

2. Which of these occupations will probably employ fewer people in the future than today?

   A. security guards   B. cashiers   C. computer operators

3. The number of employees in which of these jobs will probably increase the most?

   A. retail salespeople   B. office clerks   C. waiters

4. The number of employees in which of these jobs will probably decrease the most?

   A. textile operators   B. order clerks   C. telephone operators

All-Star 4 Study Guide

Student Name _____ Date _____

Instructor Name _____

Past Unreal Conditional Statements

Use past unreal conditional statements to talk about imaginary or unreal situations in the past. To form these statements, use the past perfect in the *if* clause and *would have* + the past participle of the verb in the main clause.

| If clause | Main clause |

If Sam **had gotten** the job, he **would have stayed** in California.
(Sam didn't get the job and he didn't stay in California.)

EXAMPLES:

If Rita and Marie **had applied** on time, they **would have gotten** the jobs.
(They didn't apply on time, and they didn't get the jobs.)

If Jim **hadn't lied** on his application, he **would have gotten** the job.
(Jim did lie, and he didn't get the job.)

Taka **wouldn't have lost** her job if she **had been** more cooperative.
(She wasn't cooperative, and she lost her job.)

3 Complete the Sentences

Complete each sentence with the correct form of the verbs in parentheses.

1. If Donna _____ *had had* _____ more supervisory experience, she would have gotten the job. (have)
2. If Jon had resolved the customer's complaint, she _____ to see his supervisor. (not ask)
3. If Sam had taken care of the company's tools, he _____ his job. (not lose)
4. If she _____ more courteous to customers, she would have gotten the promotion. (be)
5. If I _____ how to use a cash register, I would have gotten the job right away. (know)
6. If someone _____ me, I wouldn't have left the store without buying anything. (assist)
7. If she had ordered the supplies on time, they _____ by now. (arrive)
8. If the supervisor had given clear instructions, we _____ them. (follow)

4 Write

Complete each sentence with your own ideas.

1. If _____, I wouldn't have gotten angry.
2. If _____, they wouldn't have fired him.
3. If _____, I would have gone to Hawaii.
4. If _____, I would have bought a new house.
5. I wouldn't have taken the job if _____.
6. I would have gotten the job if _____.
7. She wouldn't have lost her job if _____.

All-Star 4 Study Guide

Student Name _____   Date _____

Instructor Name _____

Demonstrate understanding of job specifications, policies, standards, benefits, W2 and W4 forms. Complete sample W4 form; wages, deductions, and timekeeping forms. Student Book page 140. LCP-E 69.05 . . . CASAS 4.1.1, 4.2.1, 4.2.3, 4.4.4

1 Warm Up

Work with your classmates to answer the questions below.

1. What kinds of information appears on a pay stub?
2. What kinds of things are often deducted from a paycheck?

2 Read and Respond

Read the information on the pay stub below and answer the questions that follow.

ATWOOD INDUSTRIES

Employee: Osualdo Vargas   Check Number: 947930
Social Security Number: 123-45-6789
Pay Period Date: 3/1/05 to 3/15/05
Check Date: 3/20/05

EARNINGS	Rate	Hours	This Period	Year to Date
	20.00	80	1,600.00	8,000.00
GROSS PAY			1,600.00	8,000.00

DEDUCTIONS		
Federal Income Tax	208.00	1,040.00
Social Security	176.00	880.00
Medicare	41.60	208.00
CA Income Tax	48.22	241.10
CA State Disability Ins.	22.40	112.00
Total Deductions	496.22	2,481.10
NET PAY	1,103.78	

QUESTIONS

1. How much is Osualdo's take home pay this pay period?
2. How much money was deducted from his paycheck this pay period?
3. How often does he get a paycheck?
4. How much did he earn from January 1 to March 1?
5. How much federal income tax has he paid this year?

All-Star 4 Study Guide

Student Name _____   Date _____

Instructor Name _____

See Student Book page 140.

3 Apply

When you get a paycheck, it's important to check it over carefully. Look at Osualdo's pay stub on the right and fill in the missing numbers. You can look at the pay stub on page 140 to help you. Then compare ideas with your classmates.

ATWOOD INDUSTRIES

Employee: Osualdo Vargas   Check Number: 947941
Social Security Number: 123-45-6789
Pay Period Date: 3/16/05 to 3/31/05
Check Date: 4/5/05

EARNINGS	Rate	Hours	This Period	Year to Date
	20.00	40		
GROSS PAY				

DEDUCTIONS

Federal Income Tax	104.00		1,144.00
Social Security	88.00		
Medicare	20.80		228.80
CA Income Tax	24.11		
CA State Disability Ins.	11.20		123.20
Total Deductions			2729.21
NET PAY			

WINDOW ON MATH
Understanding Rates

A Read the information.

A *rate* is a comparison of 2 measurements that is expressed as a fraction, where the 2 measurements have different units, such as: $30/5 hours.

A *unit rate* is the rate in which the bottom number (or *denominator*) is 1: $6/1 hour. You can convert a rate to a unit rate if you divide the top number (or *numerator*) by the denominator: $30 divided by 5 hours = $6 for 1 hour.

EXAMPLE: Tina was charged $40 in bank fees on her checking account for the first four months of 2005. The rate was $40/4 months. The unit rate was $10 per month.

B Change the following rates to unit rates.

1. $5 for two hours: _____ per hour
2. 12 sick days per year: _____ per month
3. $30 for 6 months: _____ per month
4. $9 for 3 pounds: _____ per pound

C Solve the following.

1. Henry is thinking of changing jobs. At his current job, he works 40 hours and earns $500 a week. At his new job, Henry would earn $15 an hour. At which job, would Henry make more money? _____
2. Paula drives to work every day. She notices that she can go about 500 miles on a tank of gas. Her tank holds 20 gallons. What is the unit rate? _____

All-Star 4 Study Guide

Student Name _____ Date _____

Instructor Name _____

---

2 Listen and Check 🎧 _____

Read questions 1 to 9. Then listen to a conversation between a bank officer and a customer. Check (✓) 4 questions the customer asks.

3 Listen and Take Notes 🎧 _____

Listen again and add the missing information to the chart.

4 Write _____

Complete the sentences with information from the chart.

1. Neither the Green Account nor the Basic Account
   _____.

2. Both the Circle and Basic Accounts _____
   _____.

3. Unlike the Circle Account, the Green Account _____
   _____.

4. Both the Green and Basic Accounts _____
   _____.

5. All three accounts _____.

Seattle Banking	Circle Checking Account	Green Checking Account	Basic Checking Account
1. ☐ How much money do I need to open a checking account?	$50		
2. ☐ Does this account earn interest?		No	
3. ☐ Will I be charged to use the ATM at other banks?			
4. ☐ Does this account provide free checks?		N/A*	
5. ☐ How much is the monthly maintenance fee?			
6. ☐ How much do I have to keep in my account to avoid a monthly maintenance fee?		N/A	N/A
7. ☐ Does a free ATM or debit card come with this account?	Yes		
8. ☐ Does this account provide free online banking?			
9. ☐ Can I pay my bills online free of charge?			

*N/A means *not applicable*, or the question doesn't apply to this account.

Demonstrate understanding of banking system, (loans, interest rates, investments, mortgages) terms, foreign currencies and exchange rates. *BEST Plus:* State opinion about how banks encourage credit card use. State opinion about use of credit cards. Student Book pages 134–135. LCP-E 76.01 ... CASAS 1.8.1, 1.8.2, 1.8.4 ... BEST Plus

BEST *Plus:* Do you think that it's good that banks encourage the use of credit cards? Do you think it is a good idea to use a credit card or ATM card?

All-Star 4 Study Guide

Student Name _____   Date _____

Instructor Name _____

Demonstrate understanding of banking system (loans, interest rates, investments, mortgages), terms, foreign currencies, and exchange rates. BEST Plus: State opinion about how banks encourage credit card use. State opinion about use of credit cards. Student Book page 142. LCP-E 76.01 . . . CASAS 1.8.1, 1.8.2, 1.8.4 . . . BEST Plus

1 Listening Review 🎧

Listen and choose the sentence that is closest in meaning to the sentence you hear. Use the Answer Sheet.

1. A. Their biggest expense is housing.
   B. Thirty percent of their income goes for housing.
   C. They budgeted $900.00 for housing.

2. A. She has a no-fee credit card.
   B. She refuses to pay a fee for her credit card.
   C. Her credit card has an annual fee.

3. A. John owns a company that makes medicines.
   B. John owns shares of stock in a company.
   C. John works for a company that makes medicines.

4. A. Sue has invested in an individual retirement account.
   B. Every year Sue pays taxes on her income.
   C. Sue frequently puts money in her savings account.

5. A. Carlos didn't pay his credit card bill because he forgot.
   B. When Carlos forgot to pay his credit card bill, he had to pay a fee.
   C. Carlos paid a penalty fee when he received his credit card.

ANSWER SHEET

1	A	B	C
2	A	B	C
3	A	B	C
4	A	B	C
5	A	B	C
6	A	B	C
7	A	B	C
8	A	B	C
9	A	B	C
10	A	B	C

Listen to each conversation and choose the best answer to the question you hear. Use the Answer Sheet.

6. A. Put it in a savings account.
   B. Buy a certificate of deposit.
   C. Buy some stock.

7. A. a free ATM card
   B. a free check
   C. an account with free checks

8. A. fifty dollars
   B. fifteen dollars
   C. five dollars

9. A. Buy a new TV set over the phone.
   B. Get a credit card.
   C. Give out his credit card number.

10. A. the interest rate on a CD
    B. the interest rate on a savings account
    C. the interest rate on a student loan

BEST *Plus:* Do you think that it's good that banks encourage the use of credit cards? Do you think it is a good idea to use a credit card or ATM card?

All-Star 4 Study Guide

Student Name _____   Date _____

Instructor Name _____

A Look at the items Sandy bought yesterday. Write the amounts in the appropriate places on her monthly expense record below.

$45.00 $3.79 $2.50 $8.50 $6.75

TRANSPORT.		FOOD		ENTERTAIN.		MISC.		CLOTHING	
5/1 bus pass	$40.00	5/3 groceries	$275.00	5/10 concert	$32.00	5/5 books	$33.80	5/6 skirt	$38.00
5/16 parking	$6.00	5/12 lunch	$11.50	5/12 video	$4.25	5/11 shampoo	$3.00	5/6 T-shirt	$15.00
5/24 taxi	$7.30	5/22 groceries	$25.00	5/26 video	$4.25	5/16 cards	$5.75	5/20 jacket	$59.00
5/27		5/27		5/27		5/27		5/27	
Total =		Total =		Total =		Total =		Total =	

B Answer the questions about Sandy's purchases and budget.

1. Sandy budgeted $50 for entertainment this month. Is her actual spending over or under budget now? _____

2. She has a monthly spending goal of $200 or less on clothes. What will she have to do to meet this goal? _____

3. If Sandy wanted to reduce her spending, what do you think she could have done without? _____

4. Approximately what percentage of Sandy's total expenses so far this month has been spent on food? _____

C Classify the following expenses into fixed (the same every month) or variable (can change every month) expenses.

mortgage payment	school loan payments	groceries	car payments
gas	utilities	child care	clothing
health insurance	rent	entertainment	bus pass

FIXED	VARIABLE

Identify budget-planning strategies. Workbook pages 142–143. LCP-E 76.02 . . .CASAS 1.5.1, 1.5.2, 4.7.1

All-Star 4 Study Guide

Student Name _____   Date _____

Instructor Name _____

A Preview the article below and check (✓) the questions you think it will answer.

❑ What are some types of consumer fraud that immigrants may experience?

❑ How can immigrants avoid becoming victims of fraud?

❑ What are the possible punishments someone committing fraud might face?

❑ How are immigrants different from other consumers?

B Read the article and complete the sentences with words from the box.

| black market | bogus | credit | crooks | fees |
| fortunately | guard | security | fraud | |

Immigrants and Consumer Fraud

Immigrants may be more likely to become victims of _____ than other consumers because of language problems and unfamiliarity with the American market. Most Americans are aware of the services available to help them and can avoid becoming victims, but many new immigrants don't know basic consumer protection information. _____ can take advantage of immigrants in the following areas.

Credit offers: Newcomers often need to establish _____ so they can buy a car or rent an apartment. Dishonest people may offer to help an immigrant get credit, but they will charge a high fee.

Employment agencies: Some so-called "agencies" provide _____ job listings for a fee. Not only are the job leads false, the companies themselves may not exist.

Private specialized schools: Many for-profit schools design classes to attract the working immigrant. They promise to teach English and other marketable job skills, but such schools may cost a lot and deliver little.

Money wiring: Another way businesses take advantage of immigrants is to offer money transfers for very high _____. Immigrants often send money to families in other countries, and don't always have bank accounts, so they can be victimized by these businesses.

Used car sales: Immigrants often lack the English skills necessary to read and understand contracts. However, they do need cars to get to work. Dishonest used car salespeople can take advantage of this situation by charging higher prices and interest rates.

Immigrants can best _____ against these kinds of fraud by becoming educated. Adult education programs and community agencies should provide information on fraud.

All-Star 4 Study Guide

Student Name _____   Date _____

Instructor Name _____

See Workbook page 148.

C Answer these questions about the article on page 148.

1. Why do criminals often select immigrants as the targets of fraud?

   _____

2. Why do some immigrants use very high-priced money wiring services?

   _____

3. What are some ways that knowing more English could help immigrants guard against fraud?

   _____

4. What are some types of fraud that immigrants may experience?

   _____

5. How can communities help reduce these kinds of fraud?

   _____

D Choose one of the questions below. Write a paragraph about your experience.

1. Have you or someone you know been the victim of consumer fraud? If so, what happened?

2. What problems have you experienced because you are an immigrant or because of your English skills?

_____

_____

_____

_____

_____

_____

_____

_____

_____

_____

_____

_____

_____

_____

Identify ways of preventing common crimes (i.e. rape, burglary, domestic assault, car theft, etc.). Workbook page 149. LCP-E 78.02 . . . CASAS 1.6.2, 3.4.2, 3.5.9, 5.3.7, 5.3.8...BEST *Plus*

All-Star 4 Study Guide

Student Name _____   Date _____

Instructor Name _____

See Workbook page 154.

Read and discuss information related to current events. Workbook page 155. LCP-E 80.05 . . . CASAS 2.6.2, 2.7.6, 6.8.1

C Answer these questions.

1. If the government collects $1.9 trillion dollars and spends $2 trillion in one year, does it have a surplus or a deficit? _____

2. Let's say that the government spends $2 trillion in one year. If 10% of its expenses are used to pay interest on the national debt, how much money is that? _____

3. Let's say that your expenses for one year came to $30,000. If 15% of your expenses went to paying interest on your debt, how much money would that be? _____

4. What does the chart below tell you about the U.S. national debt? Write 3 things.

   1) _____

   2) _____

   3) _____

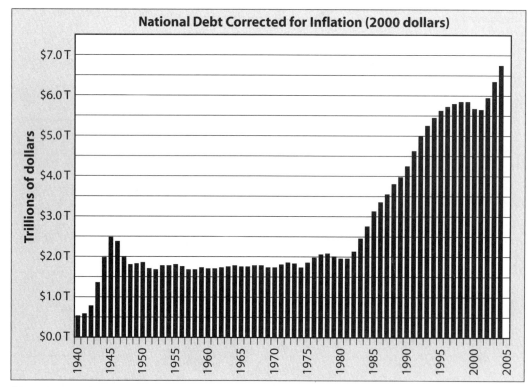

"National Debt Corrected for Inflation (2000 dollars)," U.S. National Debt Clock at www.brillig.com. Image courtesy of Ed Hall.

 TAKE IT ONLINE: Use your favorite search engine to look for the U.S. National Debt Clock. Write the current amount of the national debt in the box below.

$ _____

All-Star 4 Study Guide

Student Name _____   Date _____

Instructor Name _____

A Read the story and answer the questions below.

Develop awareness of acceptable/unacceptable parenting and disciplinary practices. Workbook page 152. LCP-E 82.03 ... CASAS 3.5.7

Financial Literacy for Kids: Money Lessons Should Start Young
by Gregory Keer

Growing up in a southeast Los Angeles neighborhood, Alicia Mendiola and her siblings were raised in a household where frugality[1] ruled. Her parents, Mexican immigrants, didn't have much money and knew that living within their means[2] meant a brighter future for their large family.

"My father had pride in having perfect credit and never bought what he could not afford," says Mendiola. "Fast food was a luxury. Everyone took turns getting new shoes, and sometimes your turn never came. After years of living in housing projects, my father bought us a home because he had good credit."

Mendiola learned from her parents' attitude towards money. The single mother struggled[3] to put herself through college and support her daughter, Irene. But today Mendiola is an assistant professor of child development at East Los Angeles College and owns a condominium in Pasadena. Despite the temptation[4] of easy credit[5], Mendiola never got into debt.

Mendiola taught her own daughter the same lesson. Once Irene entered college, Mendiola gave her daughter a fixed amount of money to spend. The budget taught her daughter how to "prioritize her purchases," she says.

---

[1] frugality: being very careful about money
[2] living within their means: not spending more money than they had
[3] struggled: worked very hard
[4] temptation: desire for something
[5] easy credit: money that is easy to borrow

"Financial Literacy for Kids: Money Lessons Should Start Young," by Gregory Keer from *L.A. Parent* at http://losangeles.parenthood.com. Used by permission of the author.

1. What lessons did Alicia's parents teach her about money?

   _____

2. How did they teach her these lessons?

   _____

3. How were her parents frugal?

   _____

4. How do you think Alicia avoided getting into debt while she was in college?

   _____

5. What lesson about money did Alicia teach her daughter?

   _____

6. How did Alicia teach her daughter this lesson?

   _____

All-Star 4 Study Guide

Student Name _____   Date _____

Instructor Name _____

Develop awareness of acceptable/unacceptable parenting and disciplinary practices. Workbook page 153. LCP-E 82.03 . . . CASAS 3.5.7

B Answer the questions below with information about yourself.

1. What was one thing you learned about money from your parents?

   _____

2. How did your parents teach you this lesson?

   _____

3. What is the most important thing parents should teach their children about money?

   _____

4. How could you teach children to "prioritize their purchases"?

   _____

5. What do you think schools should teach children about money?

   _____

 TAKE IT ONLINE: Use your favorite search engine to look for parenting magazines. Look for 3 articles with ideas for teaching children about money. Write down the titles of the articles and then discuss them with your classmates. Evaluate the titles to determine which article would be most interesting, then read that article.

All-Star 4 Study Guide

Student Name _____   Date _____

Instructor Name _____

Utilize new vocabulary by context. Workbook page 144. LCP-E 83.06

A Complete the sentences with a word or phrase from the box.

certificate of deposit	deficit	penalty	fixed	maxed out
perks	set back	shares	specific	stock

1. The interest rate on a _____ is higher than on a regular savings account.

2. That new car _____ me _____ a few thousand dollars.

3. Although adjustable rate mortgages are cheaper right now, in the long run a _____ rate mortgage might save you more money and it's predictable.

4. There's a _____ for bouncing checks.

5. I couldn't buy the video game. I _____ my credit card.

6. Downtown Bank is offering _____ to customers who open accounts this month.

7. His grandparents left him _____ of _____ in a Fortune 500 company.

All-Star 4 Study Guide

Student Name _____   Date _____

Instructor Name _____

A Read the questions in the chart below and predict the answers. Then read the information below the chart and look for the answers to the questions.

Questions	My answers before reading the text	My answers after reading the text
1) What is the European Union?		
2) When did Europe go to a single currency?		
3) Which economy has the highest unemployment, the E.U. or the U.S.?		
4) Which economy has the highest inflation rate, the E.U. or the U.S.?		

A Tale of Two Economies

In 1992 the Treaty of Maastricht instituted new forms of cooperation between members of the European Economic Community, thereby establishing a single economic system known as the European Union. It was also the year that Europe adopted a single currency, the Euro. Originally the E.U. was a partnership of 15 member nations, but 10 new countries joined in 2004. In eliminating trade and employment barriers, the E.U. created a single market that threatened to dominate the American economy.

Has that happened? Not yet, according to 2003 figures. The E.U. of 25 countries has a much larger population, although it is smaller in size. The United States imports a greater percentage of the world's imports (22.9%) than does the E.U. (14%), while the two economies are similar in their shares of world exports (13.8% and 13.1%). Stronger economies generally export more than they import. This would suggest that the E.U. has the advantage.

Other economic indicators tell a different story, however. In general, a relatively low rate of inflation and unemployment signals a healthy economy. The inflation rate in the E.U. was 2%, but only 1.6% in the United States. The rate of unemployment in the United States was 6.0%, whereas in the E.U. it was 9.1%. These figures suggest that the U.S. is still stronger economically according to these measures.

Although the single market of the European Union has given member nations definite advantages economically over the old multiple economies, time will tell if this new market is strong enough to overtake the economy of the United States.

World import share
EU 14%   US 22.9%

World export share
EU 13.1%   US 13.8%

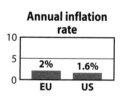

Annual inflation rate
EU 2%   US 1.6%

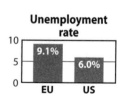

Unemployment rate
EU 9.1%   US 6.0%

All-Star 4 Study Guide

Student Name _____   Date _____

Instructor Name _____

Interpret statistical information from diagrams, tables, graphs, charts, and schedules. Workbook page 154. LCP-E 83.13 . . . CASAS 6.6.5

A What do you think? Read the statements below and check (✓) *True* or *False* in column 2.

Statements	My answers before reading the article		My answers after reading the article	
	True	False	True	False
1. The U.S. government is in debt now.	☐	☐	☐	☐
2. The U.S. government owes money to other countries.	☐	☐	☐	☐
3. The U.S. government has to pay interest on the national debt.	☐	☐	☐	☐
4. The amount of interest the government pays on the national debt is almost as much as the government pays for defense.	☐	☐	☐	☐
5. The U.S. national debt is the same as the U.S. budget deficit.	☐	☐	☐	☐

B Read the information below to check your answers from Activity A. Then check (✓) the correct answers in column 3 above.

The U.S. National Debt

On February 11, 2005, the National Debt of the United States was $7,629,320,147,691.17. That was the total amount of money that the government owed. It's a lot of money! If each person in the United States had to pay an equal share of the debt, it would cost each of us $25,812.86. So who exactly do we owe all this money to? According to the pie chart below, the largest amount of money is owed to the Federal Reserve Bank and to other government accounts. In other words, it's money we borrowed from ourselves. But it's money either we or future generations have to pay back.

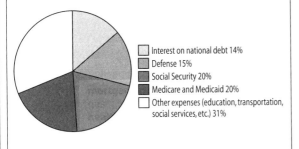

- Interest on national debt 14%
- Defense 15%
- Social Security 20%
- Medicare and Medicaid 20%
- Other expenses (education, transportation, social services, etc.) 31%

The U.S. Budget Deficit

In 2002 the U.S. government collected about $1.9 trillion in taxes but it spent about $2 trillion. Whenever the government spends more than it collects in a year, it has a budget deficit. And where did the government spend that $2 trillion? Take a look at the chart below to see.

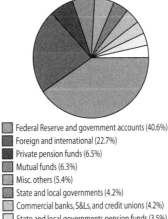

- Federal Reserve and government accounts (40.6%)
- Foreign and international (22.7%)
- Private pension funds (6.5%)
- Mutual funds (6.3%)
- Misc. others (5.4%)
- State and local governments (4.2%)
- Commercial banks, S&Ls, and credit unions (4.2%)
- State and local governments pension funds (3.5%)
- U.S. Savings bonds (3.3%)
- Insurance companies (3.3%)

"Who We Owe Money To," U.S. National Debt Clock at www.brillig.com. Images courtesy of Ed Hall.

BEST *Plus* Descriptors and Practice Questions

Unit	BEST *Plus* Descriptor	BEST *Plus* Practice Question	Study Guide Page
1	Identify self and share personal information about country of origin and current residence. Discuss learning new skills and interests. Describe learning goals and best ways to learn new things.	How long have you lived in the U.S.? Where is your family from? What are the qualities of a good learner? What new things would you like to learn? What can you do to improve your English?	1
1	Discuss emotional state of being about job interviews.	Do you get nervous during a job interview?	2
2	Describe how you choose a method of transportation.	How do you decide on a method of transportation?	16
2	Describe driving/seatbelt safety and safety of children.	Do you always wear a seatbelt?	17
3	Describe similarities and differences between going to the doctor in the U.S. versus country of origin.	Is going to the doctor in the U.S. the same or different from going to the doctor in your country?	26, 27
3	State opinion about illicit drug use among American teens and how to educate people about drugs.	How can we educate the public and children about health issues? How can we educate children and teens about the dangers of drug use?	31
4	State opinion about how children learn and what is important to learn at school.	Where do the children in your area go to school? What do you think are the most important things children learn at school? Should parents be actively involved in their children's education? What is your opinion on that topic?	44, 45
5	Describe preferences and methods of payment. Describe shopping preferences and state opinion about buying clothes.	How do you pay for your purchases (ATM, credit card, check, cash)?	51
5	Describe shopping preferences, payment, how TV and newspaper advertisements influence shopping decisions.	Do you like to go shopping? Do you think advertisements on TV and in the newspaper influence what you buy?	54, 55
6	State opinion about the degree to which violence on television may promote violent behavior	Do you think violence on television can promote violent behavior? Why?	70
6	Describe whether or not parental involvement in a child's education helps children.	Do you think a parent should be involved in a child's education? Why?	72, 73
7	Describe emotions or feelings about interviews.	Interviews can make a person very nervous. How do you usually feel during a job interview?	80
8	State opinion about how banks encourage credit card use. State opinion about use of credit cards.	Do you think that it's good that banks encourage the use of credit cards? Do you think it is a good idea to use a credit card or ATM card?	93, 94